ORİGAMİ
WORLD

ORIGAMI
WORLD

DIDIER BOURSIN

NORTH LIGHT BOOKS
Cincinnati, Ohio

Origami World. Published in the United States by North Light Books, an imprint of F+W Media, Inc., 4700 East Galbraith Road, Cincinnati, Ohio 45236. (800) 289-0963. First edition.

Library of Congress Cataloging-in-Publication Data available.

ISBN-13: 978-1-4403-0918-2 paperback
ISBN-10: 1-4403-0918-3 paperback

Printed in China by RR Donnelley
for David & Charles
Brunel House   Newton Abbot   Devon

Editorial board and editorial coordination: Colette Hanicotte with the help of Johana Sellem
Graphic design and layout: Either
Cover: Kelly O'Dell
Fold photography: Olivier Ploton
Model making: Anne Raynaud

Photography credits:
p.20, p.121, p.124 © iemily - Fotolia.com ; p.22, p.125, p.128 © zampa- Fotolia.com ; p.24, p.129, p.132 © Darren Hester - Fotolia.com ; p.26, p.133, p.136 © Michael Kempf - Fotolia.com ; p.28, p.137, p.140 © Traffic - Fotolia.com ; p.31, p.141, p.144 © Ibizarre - Fotolia.com ; p.34, p.145, p.148 © Kristalles - Fotolia.com ; p.36, p.110, p.149, p.152, p.309, p.312 © Baloncici - Fotolia.com ; p.39, p.153, p.156 © puentes - Fotolia.com ; p.42, p.157, p.160 © Nobilior - Fotolia.com ; p.44, p.161, p.164, p.165, p.168 © Freesurf - Fotolia.com ; p.47, p.169, p.172 © Laure-Hélène Maillet - Fotolia.com ; p.50, p.173, p.176 © Serg Zastavkin - Fotolia.com ; p.53, p.177, p.180, p.181 © Sunnydays - Fotolia.com ; p.56, p.184, p.185, p.188 © owen - Fotolia.com ; p.62, p.189, p.192 © Galina Barskaya - Fotolia.com ; p.64, p.193, p.196 © adisa - Fotolia.com ; p.66, p.197, p.200 © Nikolai Sorokin - Fotolia.com ; p.68, p.201, p.204 © Andrii Pokaz - Fotolia.com ; p.70, p.205, p.208 © Yuriy Chertok - Fotolia.com ; p.72, p.209, p.212 © FotoLyriX - Fotolia.com ; p.74, p.213, p.216 © Mickaël Berteloot - Fotolia.com ; p.76, p.120, p.217, p.220 © cphoto - Fotolia.com ; p.78, p.221, p.224 © Marek - Fotolia.com ; p.80, p.120, p.225, p.228 © cyrano - Fotolia.com ; p.82, p.229, p.232© Irochka - Fotolia.com ; p.84, p.233, p.236, p.237, p.240, p.241, p.244, p.245, p.248, p.249, p.252, p.253, p.256, p.257, p.260, p.261, p.264 © Andrii Pokaz - Fotolia.com ; p.86, p.265, p.268, p.269, p.272 © clearviewstock - Fotolia.com ; p.88, p.120, p.273, p.276 © Jennifer Stone - Fotolia.com ; p.90, p. 277, p.280, p.281, p. 284 © Adroach - Fotolia.com ; p.94, p.285, p.288 © Anette Linnea Rasmussen - Fotolia.com ; p.96, p.289, p.292 © zigrit - Fotolia.com ; p.98, p.293, p.296 © thier - Fotolia.com ; p.101, p.297, p.300 © Jimmy Lu - Fotolia.com ; p.104, p.106, p.120, p.304, p.305, p.308 © Piotr Skubisz - Fotolia.com ; p.112, p.313, p.316 © c - Fotolia.com ; p.114, p. 317, p.320 © thegarden - Fotolia.com ; p.117, p.321, p.324 © Adrian Hillman - Fotolia.com ; p.325 © Thor Jorgen Udvang - Fotolia.com ; p.328 © Viktoriia Kulish - Fotolia.com ; p. 329 © yxowert - Fotolia.com ; p.332 © Victoria Greenlees - Fotolia.com ; p.333 © mashe - Fotolia.com ; p.336 © Offscreen - Fotolia.com ; p.337 © Nikola Spasenoski - Fotolia.com ; p.340 © Liz Van Steenburgh - Fotolia.com ; p.341 © Annabelbee - Fotolia.com ; p.344 © PaulPaladin - Fotolia.com

www.fwmedia.com

Acknowledgments
I would like to thank all those who have helped me, in whatever way, with demonstrating the folds in this book. Thank you to designer Takeshi Inoué, who created the Fighter Plane model that he kindly wanted to share with me. Thank you to my photographer Olivier Ploton. Thank you to Setsuko and Simon (in her arms) for the black and white photo in the Photo Frame model. I would also like to thank the whole editorial team.

You can share your personal experiences and comments at:
www.origami-creation.com

◇◇◇ FOREWORD

Paper folding probably originated in China around the time that paper was invented. Several centuries later, it was developed in Japan and became a ceremonial art in the Shinto tradition in the form of boxes for offerings and zigzag paper folding for the gods. Paper folding then became a subtle art of packaging, using white paper to conserve spices and medicines and to wrap little, day-to-day objects, such as combs, fans and chopsticks. Paper, made on a large scale, became a more accessible product and resulted in a recognized pastime called Origami. Nowadays, throughout the world, both children and adults practise the art of paper folding, especially as contemporary designers have been able to pass on this tradition and develop it with their creations. In this book, Didier Boursin sets out around forty creations: from aeroplanes with amazing performance and very decorative animals, through to boxes that can be used on any occasion. All these different folded models can be quite surprising due to the superb coloured papers carefully chosen to achieve the best effects.

Contents

Land and sea _____

Fun and functional _____

Wings and feathers _____

Folds and symbols
> Advice

Before starting, take a look at the 'Folds and symbols' (pp. 8–11) and 'Sketches of bases and details' (pp. 12–17) sections, which explain the essential folds. These include the 'valley' fold (crease is at the bottom) and the 'mountain' fold (crease is at the top), as well as other movements and combinations of folds that will subsequently be useful.

Each fold and movement is represented in a diagram by an arrow and dots to be joined together. To avoid making any mistakes, make sure you know the difference between folding the paper and marking the crease. In the first instance, you make the fold; in the second, you crease it as indicated by the double arrow. If necessary, refer to the subsequent diagram which will also help you to understand the previous step.

At first, you should practise folding simple models in a square format using ordinary paper. The best papers are those that are no more than 90g, such as Pop'Set or Kraft. Then move on to making the animals, objects and aeroplanes in the recommended papers suggested at the end of the book (pp. 121–344), or in any other papers of your choice. You will find that the random fall of the folds makes the object look different each time.

We have marked the level of difficulty of the folds using shaded diamonds. Start out by folding easy models so that you can learn the basic terminology, acquire a light touch and achieve accuracy with your movements. Some people aren't immediately successful at paper folding, but don't let that put you off. Your second attempt will often be better than your first. For each origami model, you have two chances at succeeding with your paper folding, or in any case, enough paper to make two examples.

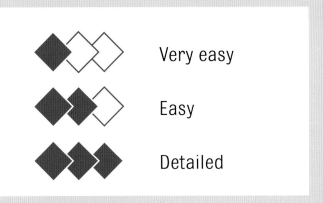

Very easy

Easy

Detailed

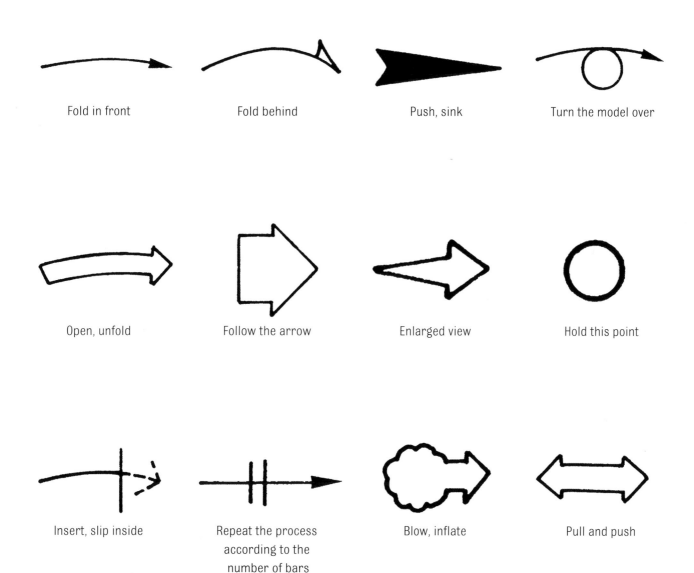

Fold in front

Fold behind

Push, sink

Turn the model over

Open, unfold

Follow the arrow

Enlarged view

Hold this point

Insert, slip inside

Repeat the process according to the number of bars

Blow, inflate

Pull and push

Folds and symbols

> Main folds

> Valley fold

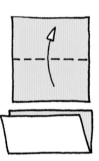

> Mountain fold

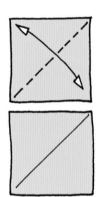

> Mark the crease

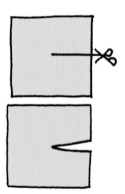

> Pleat or zigzag fold

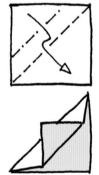

> Join the dots

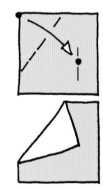

> Cut

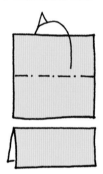

> Inside reverse fold

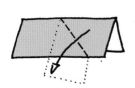 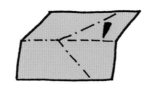 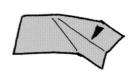

> Outside reverse fold

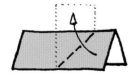 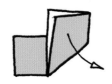 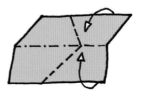 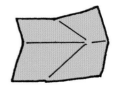

Sketches of bases and details

> Preliminary base

   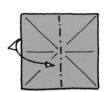

By pressing with your finger at the centre (**a**) you can obtain the Water bomb base.

> Water bomb base

  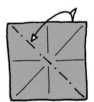 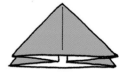

By pressing with your finger at the centre (**b**) you can obtain the Preliminary base.

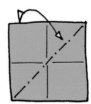 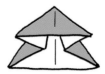

> Open sink

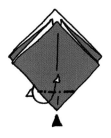 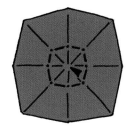  

1. To perform the fold, fold all the thicknesses in front and behind, then unfold completely.

2. Mark the central square using a mountain fold (see p. 10), then press in the centre to sink the square.

3. At the centre of the square, the diagonals are in valley fold (see p. 10) and the central creases are in mountain fold. Flatten as in Step 1.

Sketches of bases and details

> Bird base

 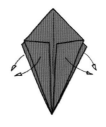  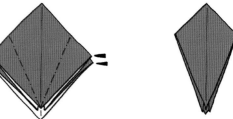

1. Fold the lower edges onto the centre fold on both sides using a preliminary base (see p. 12).

2. Unfold.

3. Push the sides in using inside reverse folds (see p. 11).

> Bird's legs

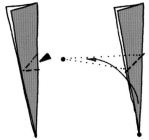 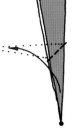 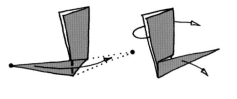 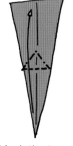 

The fold is performed in two main stages:

1. Lift up the tip horizontally.

2. Fold over to the right.

3. Unfold completely.

4. Mark the two upper sides of the triangle using mountain fold (see p. 10), then lift up the tip using the valley fold (see p. 10) of the remaining side of the triangle.

5. Fold in half by placing the sides of the triangle in mountain fold.

> Bird's beak

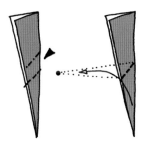 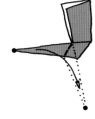   

To make this fold:

1. Lift up the tip horizontally.

2. Fold the tip back downwards. To make a beak, fold the tip more to the right, keeping it parallel.

3. Unfold completely.

4. Mark the mountain and valley folds as indicated (see p. 10), then fold in half along the vertical fold.

5. Fold flat.

Sketches of bases and details

> Fish base

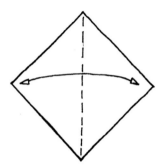

1. Mark the vertical crease.

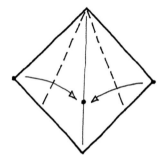

2. Fold the upper edges onto the centre crease.

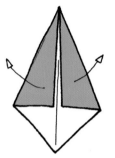

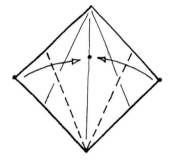

3. Unfold.

4. Fold the lower edges in the same way.

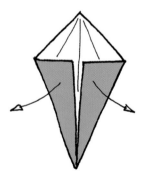

5. Unfold.

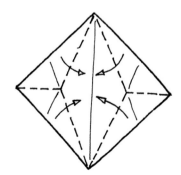

6. Fold over the edges whilst pinching the side points at the same time.

7. Flatten, placing the points upwards.

> Frog base

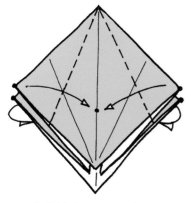

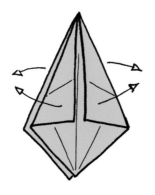

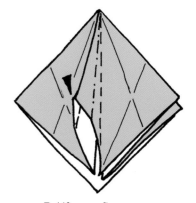

1. Fold the upper edges onto the two sides of a preliminary base (see p. 12).

2. Unfold.

3. Lift up a flap vertically and then open by squashing.

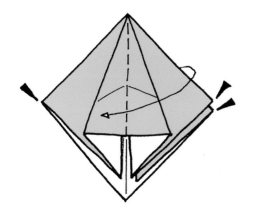

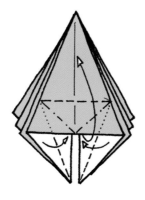

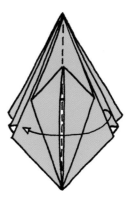

4. Repeat the same fold on the other three flaps.

5. Lift up a flap, folding the points in half.

6. Turn over a flap and repeat this fold on the other three faces.

Land and sea

Sea turtle

More at home on land than at sea, the sea turtle is admired for the beauty of its shell, presented graphically here with a striking coloured pencil print.

For recommended paper, see pp. 121 and 124

1. **Fold** down the sides to the centre, joining the dots.

2. **Fold** the top two corners, then turn over.

3. **Fold** the sides, releasing the paper underneath.

4. **Fold** the square in half.

5. **Lift up** one third, joining the dots (**1**) then, starting at the centre of the base, fold along the vertical axis (**2**).

6. **Make** the front legs by joining the dots (**1**) to reduce the head. Then fold downwards to make the back legs emerge (**2**).

7. **Give** some volume to the shell using a pleat, then turn over.

8. **Make** a pleat at tail level to hold the dorsal pleat (**1**), then shape the feet and the head.

To make the shell rounded, fold down the angles at the sides.

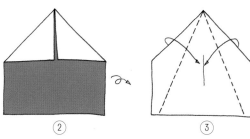

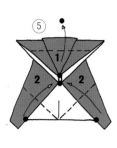

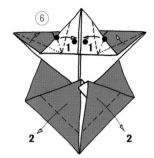

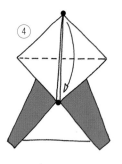

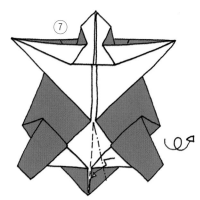

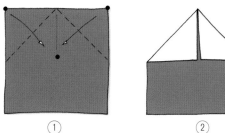

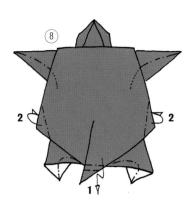

sea turtle > 21

Seal

Seals use their whiskers to give them an innate sense of balance. This crisp, aquatic paper design is evocative of their lives in the cold waters of the deep blue sea.

For recommended paper,
see pp. 125 and 128

1. **Start** with the water bomb base (see p. 12). Place an extra triangle over to the right.

2. **Lift** a triangle up along the left edge.

3. **Squash** the second layer along the right edge.

4. **Check** your model is as shown, then turn over.

5. **Repeat** the same fold as before, joining the dots.

6. **Fold down** the tips, joining the dots, then cut the tip in half for 2cm (¾in).

7. **Lift up** one of the triangles between the two layers (**1**). Then fold down the upper tip for the head (**2**).

7a **Detail for the tail.**

Details for the head

7b **Unfold** the angle completely.

7c **Fold down** the tip to create the nose (**1**). Cut the sides to make the whiskers appear (**2**), then re-fold the head in the creases, as indicated.

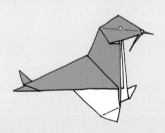

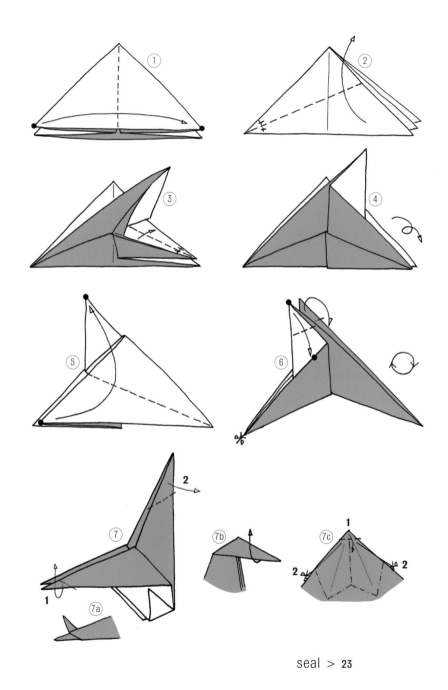

seal > **23**

Frog

This little tree frog in 'sponge' paper is all ready to croak, announcing the rain and the fine weather.

For recommended paper, see pp. 129 and 132

1. **Make** the frog base (see p. 17), then turn a flap onto each of the faces.

2. **Fold over** the sides onto the two faces.

3. **Turn** a layer onto each of the faces, to make one face become two. Fold over the sides, as in step 2, onto the two faces.

4. **Turn** a flap onto each face.

5. **For the forelegs**, lift up the tips of the upper face in a reverse fold.

6. **For the hind legs**, make an inside reverse fold (see p. 11) as on the left.

7. **Make** reverse folds for the fore and hind legs as on the left side.

8. **Fold down** the tips in a reverse fold for the four feet, then turn over.

9. **Inflate** the frog from the back. Add beads for the eyes between the layers and bend the front tip behind. Cut the tips of the feet in half.

Detail for the feet

9a. **Open** the tips of the feet and cut them in half again to make five toes.

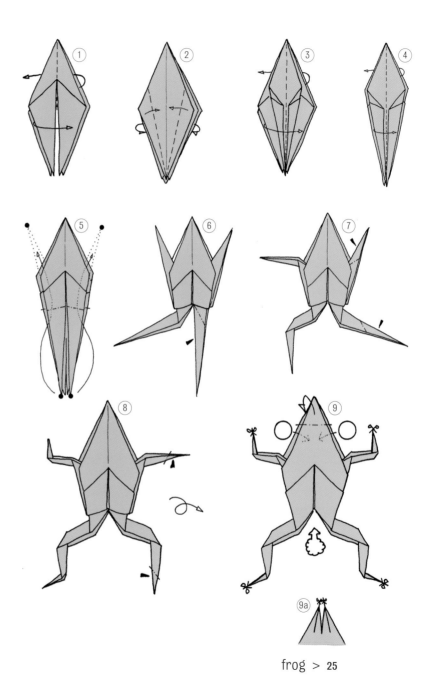

Panther

This pink panther bears a striking resemblance to the famous Hollywood cartoon character.

For recommended paper, see pp. 133 and 136

1. **Make** the fish base. Open outwards

2. **Make** a pleat.

3. **Reduce** the width of the tip by folding the sides into the centre crease and refolding everything flat.

4. **Bend** the tip behind.

5. **Open** the sides to push the base inside by making a reverse fold.

5
a-b **For the legs**, open the tips of the sides and fold the tip back onto itself towards the outside. Fold the tip in half.

6. **Mark the upper fold**. At the sides, the first layer is folded inside.

6a **Fold** inside the other layers.

6
b-c **Open** the upper tip, refold the triangle behind, then place the sides back into their creases.

7. **To make the head**, fold it down onto the side. For the ears, cut through all the layers rounding them. Push in the base of the tail with a reverse fold then fold over the end.

8. **For the whiskers**, cut out two tips on each side. Fold down the snout. Cut at the base for the chops. Flatten the ears.

8a **Lift up** the ears and bend the outside edge behind.

9. **For the eyes**, make a pleat. Fold over the corners to hold it.

10. **For the muzzle**, make a pleat and shape the arches of the eyebrows using your thumbs.

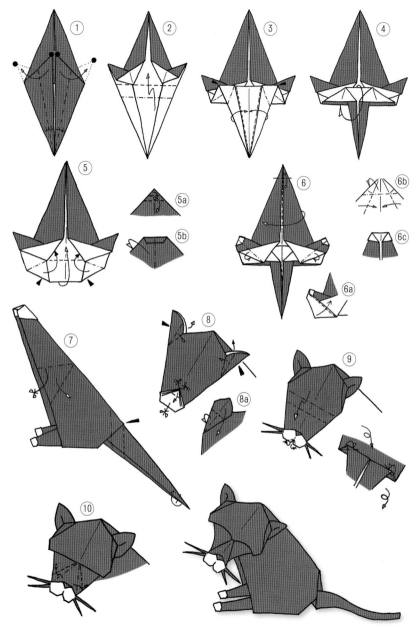

panther > 27

Fish

This paper gives the illusion that these fish are floating wherever the tide takes them, bobbing along with the current in the warm waves of the ocean.

For recommended paper, see pp. 137 and 140

1. **Join** the centre crease of a square by folding in the lower edges then unfold.

2. **Fold** the upper edges down in the same way.

3. **Lift up** the corners towards the top, refolding the sides back into their creases.

4. **Cut** along the unbroken line, then refold everything in half behind.

5. **Fold** one tip vertically downwards.

6. **Lift up** this tip on the other side.

7. **Fold** this tip towards the left.

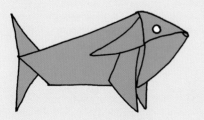

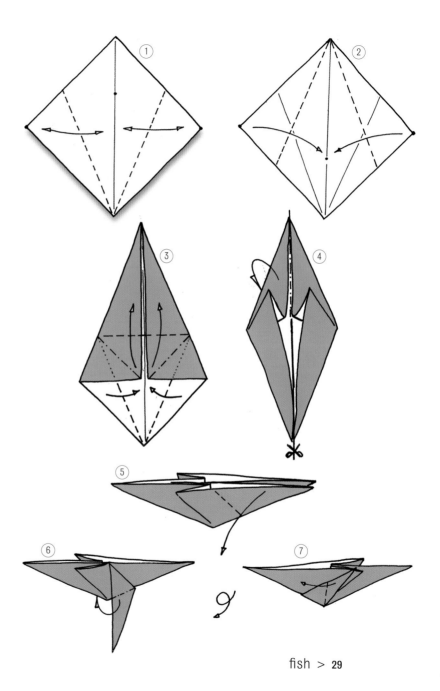

Fish (cont.)

8 **Fold** this tip towards the right.

9 **Fold** the second tip vertically downwards.

10 **Lift up** this tip on the other side and then turn over.

11 **Make** a pleat in this tip and secure it between the two layers.

12 **Fold down** vertically the underneath triangle on each side, then lift up the tip of the tail vertically.

Details for the tail

12a **Unfold.**

12b **Push** the tip into a reverse fold.

12c **Cut** this tip in half.

12d **Fold** the tip behind, as shown.

12e **Fold** the top tip downwards.

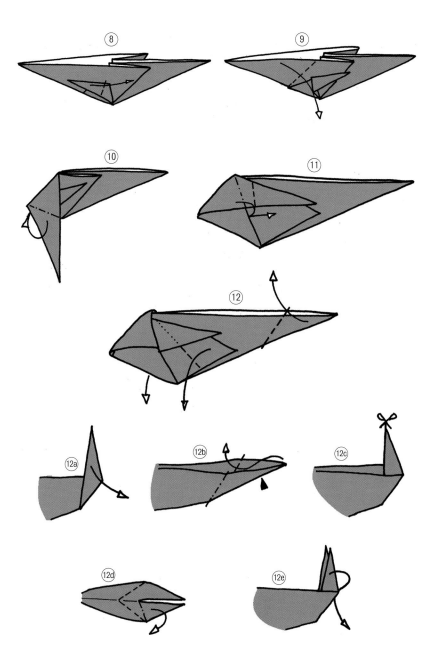

Mouse

While some mice like to scurry around all day, others – like this little untamed mouse – prefer a quiet life in the attic.

For recommended paper, see pp. 141 and 144

Mouse (cont.)

1 **Fold** the sides onto the centre crease.

2 **Arrange** as shown, then turn over.

3 **Fold** to join the dots.

4 **Fold** the sides down flat.

5 **Lift up** the sides along the vertical crease.

6 **Fold down** the top tip twice onto itself (**1**). Cut two fine bands for the whiskers (**2**), then fold down the top part towards the bottom (**3**).

7 **Fold** in half along the vertical crease.

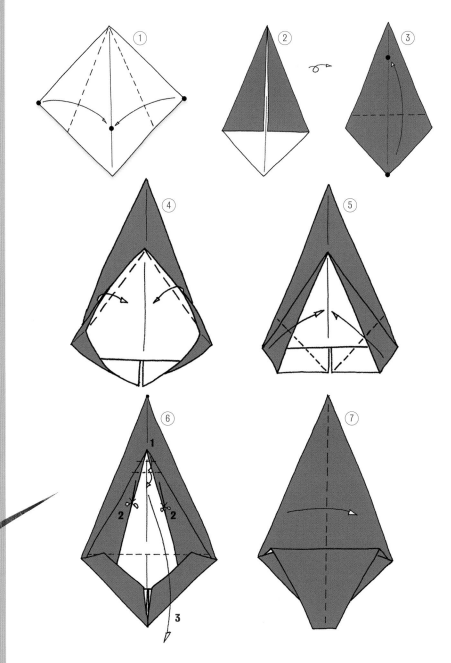

8 Prepare the creases for the ears on the right part (**1**). Unfold the whiskers. Make an inside reverse fold (see p. 11) for the tail (**2**) and make a pleat to give the mouse some volume: this pleat can be slipped between two layers inside the paper folding (**3**).

Details for the ears

8a Make a squash fold.

8b Fold in half.

8c Open one side slightly.

8d Check your model is as shown.

9 Lift up the tip in an inside reverse fold (see p. 11) by slightly opening the sides.

Details for the tail

9a Fold over the free edges to the inside to slim down the tail.

9b Bend the tail.

To make a standing mouse, fold the tail quite high at step 9, then slim it down as in step 9a.

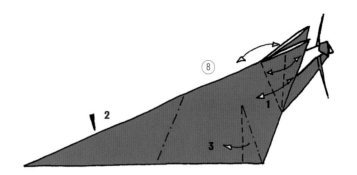

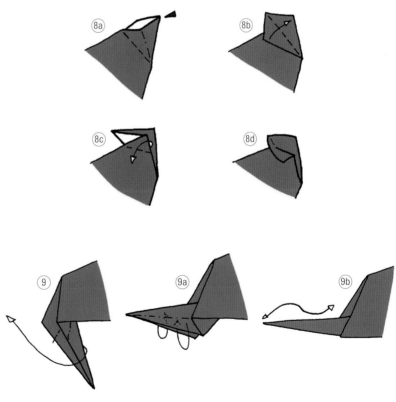

Rabbit

This rabbit made from 'furry' paper will make an adorable little pet, ideal for children.

For recommended paper, see pp. 145 and 148

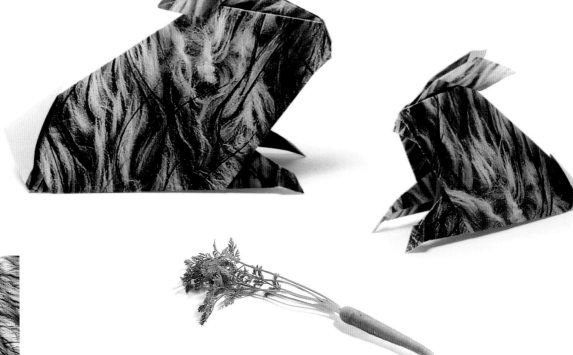

1. **Join** the sides onto the centre crease.

2. **Lift up** the bottom triangle.

3. **Fold** one third downwards joining the dots.

4. **Release** the two flaps by folding around the edge of the previous fold.

5. **Fold down** the sides, respecting the proportions.

6. **To slim down** the tips, fold down the flap, opening it along the marked creases.

7. **To make a tail**, bend the lower tip towards the back, then fold everything in half along the vertical crease.

Details for the head

8. **Make** a reverse fold after pre-creasing. For the legs, make a squash fold as for the ears (see steps 11 and 12). Separate the tail giving the body its form.

9. **Lift up** the tip inside in a reverse fold.

Details for the ears

10. **Cut** the tip in half to separate the ears. Fold over the front and fit the two flaps together to make the muzzle.

11. **Mark** the base crease of the ear, then make a squash fold.

12. **Check** your model is as shown. Shape the ears then the back to give the rabbit some volume.

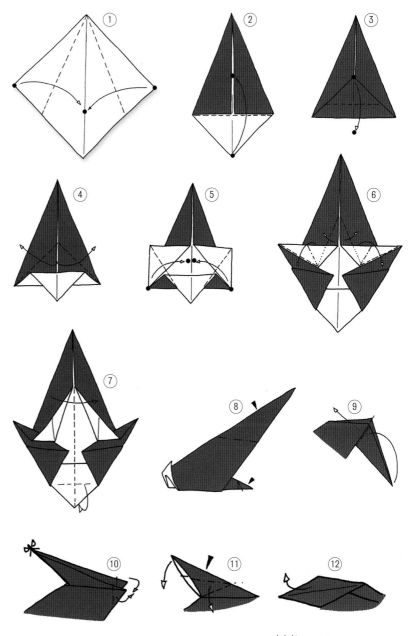

rabbit > **35**

Giraffe

Despite its size, the giraffe can be made from a single sheet of paper, in colours that evoke the African savannah.

For recommended paper, see pp. 149 and 152

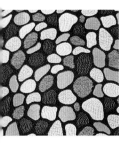

1. **Fold** a square in half.
2. **Lift up** the tips.
3. **Fold** the sides, then unfold.
4a. **Cut** two notches for the tail.
4b. **Cut** out the top layer, then unfold the tail.
5. **Lift up** the tips.
6. **Lower** the tips from the notch of the tail as on the right, refolding the little legs underneath.
7. **Check** your model is as shown, then turn over.
8. **Lift up** the tail.

Details for the tail

8a. **Fold** the sides onto the centre crease, flattening the triangle as on the left.
8b. **Check** your model is as shown.
9. **Open** apart, turning down the first layer towards the front.
10. **At the same time**, fold the sides in the marked creases (**1**) and fold the tips in half (**2**) to flatten everything.
11. **Fold** in half.

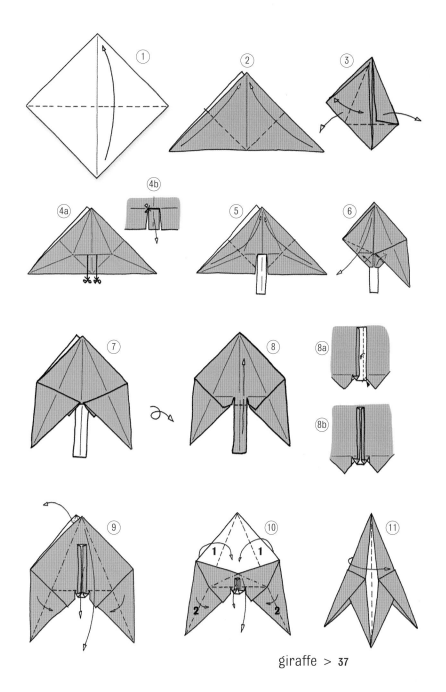

giraffe > 37

Giraffe (cont.)

12   **Make** a pleat and push it between the layers. Reverse the direction of the creases for the other face.

13   **Check** your model is as shown.

14   **Locate** the position of the head with a pleat (**1**). Cut out the ears and the horns, then separate them by cutting the centre crease (**2**). Push the end of the tip inside (**3**) then make the pleat for the head.

Details for the head

14a   **Fold** the muzzle, then flatten the head a little.

14b   **Check** your model is as shown.

Details for the tail

14c   **Lift up** the sides along a cross crease.

14d   **Fold down** the excess at the end on each side.

14e   **Check** your model is as shown, then slightly bend the tail. Give everything volume by shaping the legs and the neck.

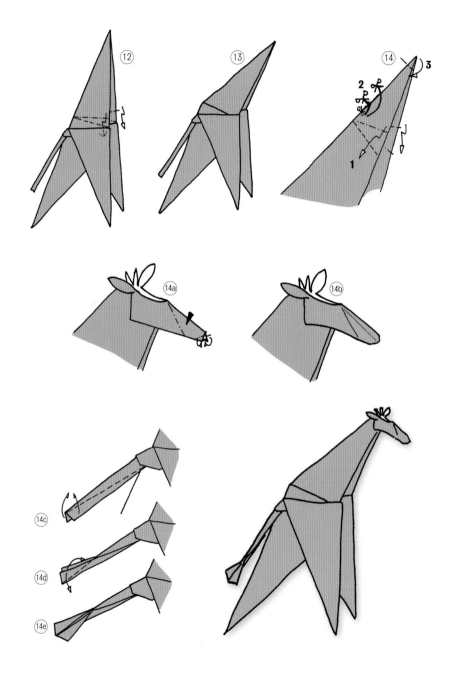

Horse

This strong horse likes trotting in the wilderness, which is suggested by the striking earthy print of this paper.

For recommended paper, see pp. 153 and 156

Horse (cont.)

1   **Fold** the sides of a preliminary base (see p. 12).

2   **Cut** along the unbroken line only on the top and bottom flaps, then unfold.

3   **Fold down** the tips of each face.

4   **Push up** the tip to the base after pre-creasing (**1**). Fold down the sides along the whole length (**2**).

5   **Locate** the position of the head at the dotted line and make a pre-crease for the tail: a right-angled crease, then a second one dividing the remaining angle in half.

Detail for the head

6   **To make the mane**, cut through all the layers of one tip. For the ears, cut through all the layers in a curve.

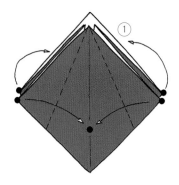

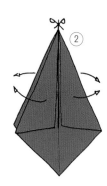

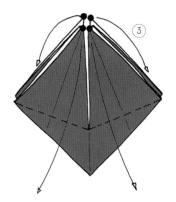

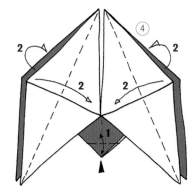

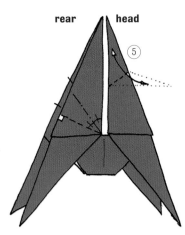

rear   head

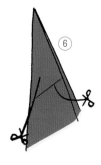

Details for the head

7 **Open** the head and make a pleat to create the nostrils.

8 **Make** the ears stand up (**1**) and refold everything in a reverse fold (**2**).

9 **Make** a pleat at the front of the head.

10 **Check** your model is as shown.

Details for the rear

11 **Open** the tip to form the rear, then lower it down into its creases on each side.

12 **Make** a pleat inside to make the tail.

Details for the tail

13 **Make** a reverse fold.

14 **Open** the sides, turning them over.

15 **Slim down** the base of the tail and shape the end with a reverse fold.

16 **To make the horse trot**, make a reverse fold in the fore and hind legs. Bend the head forwards to make a crease on each face. Give the horse some volume.

horse > 41

Elephant

We see them at zoos or circuses, but in some countries the elephant is a sacred animal. This mother and baby boast a fascinating oriental design.

For recommended paper, see pp. 157 and 160

1. **Start** with the fish base (see p. 16). Divide the angle in half, folding the tips towards the outside.

2. **By spreading** the tips, flatten the inside creases, then turn over.

3. **Mark** the creases, then fold in half along the vertical crease.

4. **Fold** the top tip in an outside reverse fold (see p. 11) after pre-creasing. Fold the left tip in an inside reverse fold (see p. 11) after pre-creasing.

5. **Push** the upper tip of the head inside. For the trunk, make a pre-crease; for the tail, make a reverse fold after pre-creasing. Fold over the tips of the forelegs by opening the ends.

5a. **Mark** the second crease of the trunk, then make a pleat inside.

5b. **Fold** the tip downwards using a pleat.

5c. **Fold** down the tips towards the inside, at the base of the elephant. Fold the tail downwards and make the back round.

To finish, shape the ears.

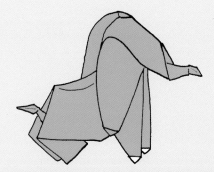

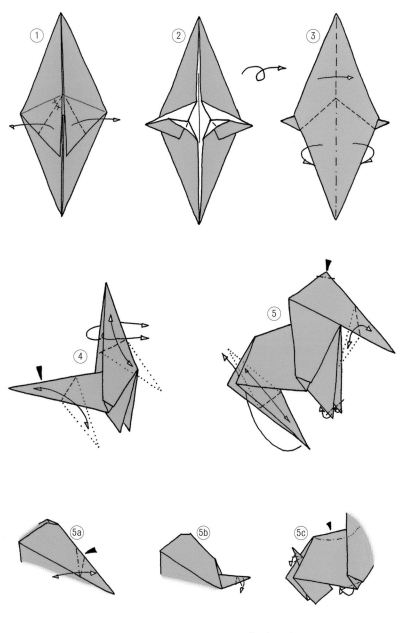

elephant > **43**

Cat

The cat is a favourite domestic pet for many. This spotted paper brings out their wild side, likening them to their larger, fiercer relative, the leopard.

For recommended paper, see pp. 161, 164, 165 and 168. Use two squares of paper

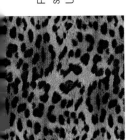

Body

1 **Fold down** a corner (**1**) then fold over in half along the diagonal (**2**).

2 **To make the tail**, fold the tip downwards.

3 **Fold** the tip in half (**1**) then unfold (**2**).

4 **Make** a reverse fold in the tip.

5 **Reverse** the creases marked on the two faces.

6 **Lift up** the tip in a reverse fold, then fold down the upper triangle.

7 **Make** a pleat on the two layers, adding volume to the piece. Then mark this pleat on the other face, reversing the direction of the pleats.

8 **Check** your model is as shown.

Head

9 **Fold** a square in half (smaller than the one used for the body).

10 **Fold** the tips downwards.

11 **To make the ears**, lift up the tips as on the right.

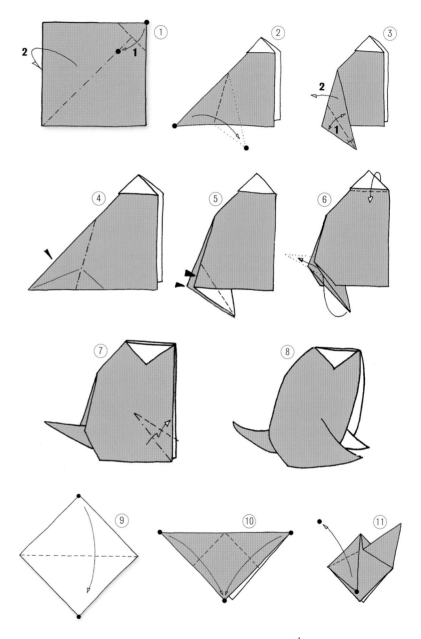

Cat (cont.)

12   **Fold over** the upper triangle, then turn over the piece.

13   **Lower** the ears, opening the sides without squashing. To make the muzzle, make a pleat, giving everything some volume, then turn over.

Details

13a   **Press** on the top of the ear, pulling the tip backwards.

13b   **Check** your model is as shown.

13c   **For the muzzle**, lift up the tip inside at a right angle.

13d   **Fold** onto the side and gently separate the two triangles.

13e   **Check** your model is as shown, then turn everything over.

14   **Reduce** the sides by folding behind. Mark the creases of the snout by pressing in the centre. Bend the ears back and shape the eyes using the thumbs. Lift up the upper triangle located behind.

15   **Slip** the triangle of the head into the top pocket of the body.

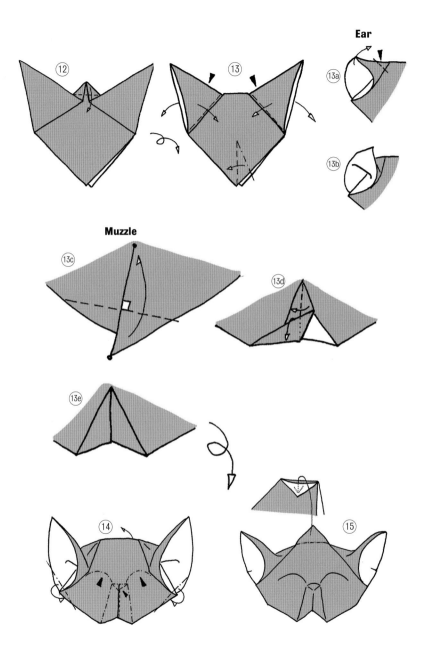

Penguin

Groups of penguins will stand proudly together on the ice, similar to this little family made from 'ice floe' paper.

For recommended paper, see pp. 169 and 172

Penguin (cont.)

1 **Mark** the centre crease, then fold down the sides onto this crease.

2 **Fold** behind.

3 **Mark** the crease turning down the tip to outline the head (**1**), then open the sides (**2**).

4 **Mark** the crease turning down all of the left part as indicated, then open completely.

5 **Before refolding**, place the valley and mountain folds as indicated.

6 **Begin** refolding from the start.

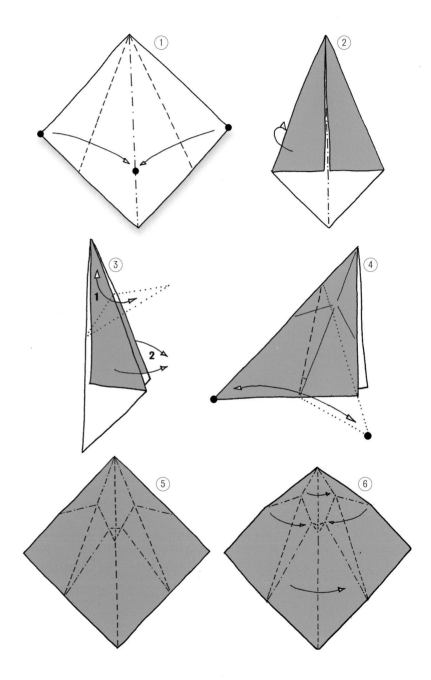

7 **Fold down** the lower part towards the left. For the beak, fold down the tip.

8 **Lift up** the tip of the beak and the lower triangle.

9 **Cut** along the unbroken line, mark the crease at the base (**1**) and then unfold the beak and the base (**2**).

10 **For the beak** and the lower triangle, open, then make reverse folds (**1**). Fold down the left part on each face to form the wings (**2**).

Detail for the beak

10a **Reduce the beak** by turning half the width inside. Fold over the end.

Detail for the feet

10b **To make the feet**, fold the base inside, then place the feet flat. Add volume to the penguin from the inside.

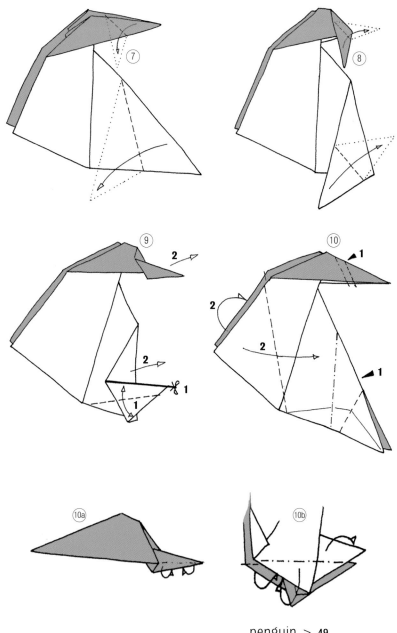

Crab

This seashore crustacean has a pair of large claws that it uses to tickle you as you pass by.

For recommended paper, see pp. 173 and 176

1. **Make** the frog base (see p. 17), then fold the tip from each side downwards.

2. **Turn** the flaps along the vertical crease to make two new triangles appear on the two faces.

3. **Lift up** the tip horizontally, then unfold.

4. **Slightly open** to slip the left tip between the layers as on the right side.

5. **To double the number of legs**, cut the centre crease of the tips in half. Move the underneath tips upwards, then turn everything over.

6. **On the four upper legs**, make outside reverse folds (see p. 11) after pre-creasing by bending the tips upwards. On the lower tips, make reverse folds after pre-creasing as on the right tip.

7. **Make** another inside reverse fold (see p. 11) on the lower tips as on the right tip.

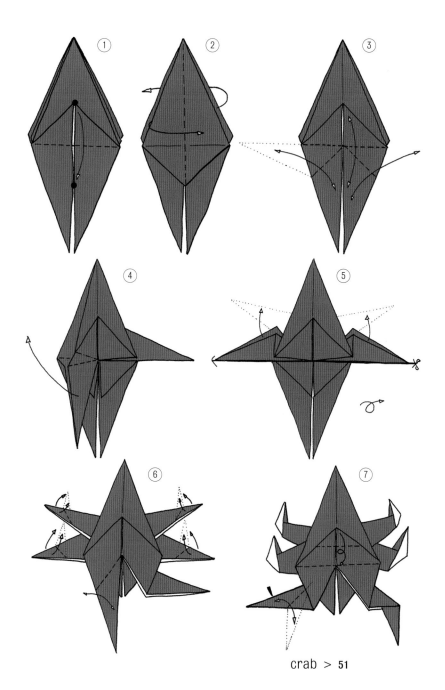

crab > 51

Crab (cont.)

8   **To make the claws**, fold one layer of the tip, bending it backwards as for the right claw (8c). For the eyes, fold down the triangles onto the top, then open the pockets to make squares.

Details

8a **Check** your model is as shown.

8b **Fold down** the sides of the squares curving the eyes.

8c **Turn over** the whole piece as shown.

9   **Fold over** the tip towards the left to make the hollow shell.

10 **Bend** the tip towards the top.

11 **Open** the left side of this tip.

12 **To retain** the volume, push the free parts between the layers of the central triangle. Turn over.

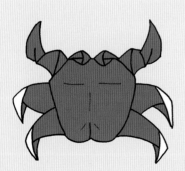

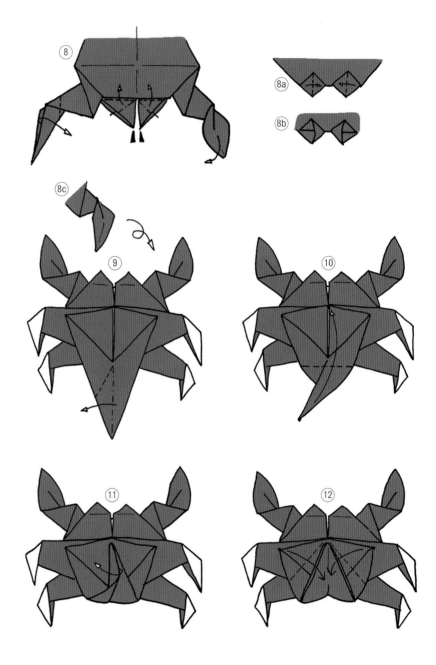

Bull

This bull is proudly displaying its lively, Mediterranean colours. Here, he is completely harmless, in contrast to the symbol of great power that he represents.

For recommended paper, see pp. 177, 180 and 181. Use two squares of paper

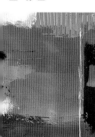

Bull (cont.)

Body

1. **Fold** a square along the diagonal (slightly larger than that of the head), then lift up the tips of the sides, joining the dots.

2. **Mark** the creases on all the layers dividing the tips in half, then unfold.

3. **Make** reverse folds on both sides.

4. **Make** reverse folds in the four corners by following the pre-creasing.

5. **Pull down** a flap.

6. **Pull down** the tips in a reverse fold by slightly opening the sides. Fold the lower triangle.

7. **Fold** the triangles down behind, then turn over.

8. **Pinch** the upper tip. This is where the head will go.

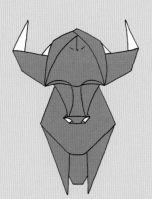

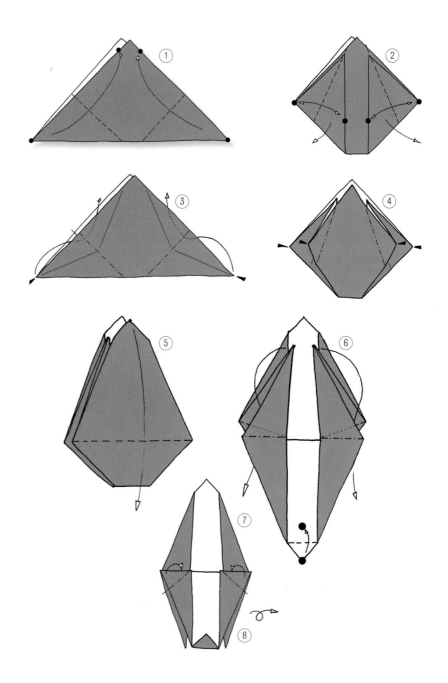

Head

9. **Lift up** the tips of an isosceles triangle, joining the dots.

10. **Mark** the creases on all the layers, dividing the tips, then unfold.

11. **Fold down** the tips towards the outside from the central dot of the previous step, then fold over the upper triangle.

12. **Fold down** the left side into its creases then turn over.

13. **Fold over** the other side in the same way.

14. **Make** a pleat, pushing the corners between the layers, then turn over.

15. **Open** the two flaps turning them down onto the sides. To make the horns, make reverse folds after pre-creasing.

16. **Mark** the base of the horns with a pleat; then give some volume to the head by making a pleat on the top part that will be held in place between the layers.

Details

16a. **Fold down** behind the tip that sticks out. This slightly open tip will enable the head to be held on to the body.

17. **To finish the muzzle**, bend the base, then bend the flap to the front. Shape the eyes by pressing on the horizontal edge and by unfolding the pleat. Place the head onto the body.

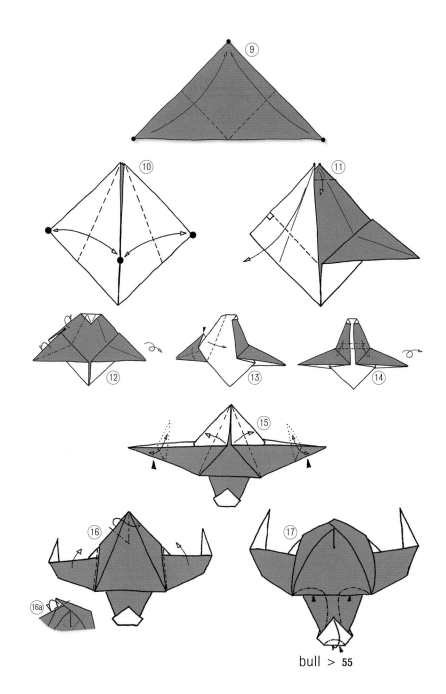

bull > **55**

Monkey

The baboon is an acrobatic little monkey that is found in zoos all over the world. He amuses children with his faces and mannerisms. This one surprises us with his fabulous coat.

For recommended paper, see pp. 184, 185 and 188. Use two squares of paper

Top part

1 **Lift up** the tips of an isosceles triangle (see step 8, p. 58) placing the coloured side down. Fold (**1**) the sides into the centre crease, then unfold completely (**2**).

2 **Place** the creases in the right direction, then lift up the tips.

3 **To make the upper limbs**, fold the left tip in such a way that it is higher than the right tip.

4 **Reduce** the width of the arms by folding them in half. Mark the crease of the upper tip, perform steps 4a to 4c, then fold everything in half.

Detail for the arm

4a **Fold** the left arm upwards in an outside reverse fold (see p. 11).

Details for the muzzle

4 b-c **To make the muzzle**, open the upper tip, fold the triangle behind, then fold over into its creases.

5 **To make the head**, fold onto the side by turning down the top.

Details for the hands

5a **Open** the upper limb, make the creases as indicated, then fold over in half.

5b **Open** the other limb, make the creases, then fold over in half.

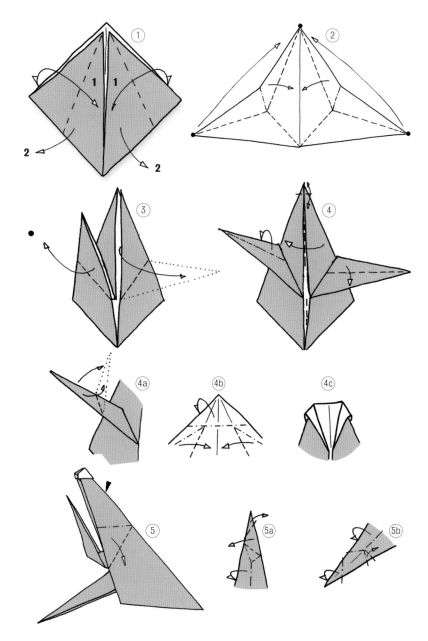

Monkey (cont.)

6   **Push in** the tip of the base with a reverse fold (**1**). To make the ears, make reverse fold pleats (**2**). For the muzzle, fold the triangle (**3**).

7   **To make the eyes**, use triangular creases (**1**). For the muzzle, make a pleat on each side (**2**). Round off the muzzle (**3**).

Lower part

8   **Lift up** the tips of an isosceles triangle.

9   **Mark** the creases turning down the sides onto the centre crease.

10 **Fold down** the tips towards the outside as on the right, folding in half towards the outside, then turn over.

11 **Mark** all the creases, then start to fold down the sides to the centre (**1**) and the tips onto themselves (**2**).

12 **Flatten** the triangle as on the right, by pulling the raised part, sliding a finger between the layers and gently flattenning as on the right part.

13 **To make the legs**, make a reverse fold after pre-creasing, then turn over.

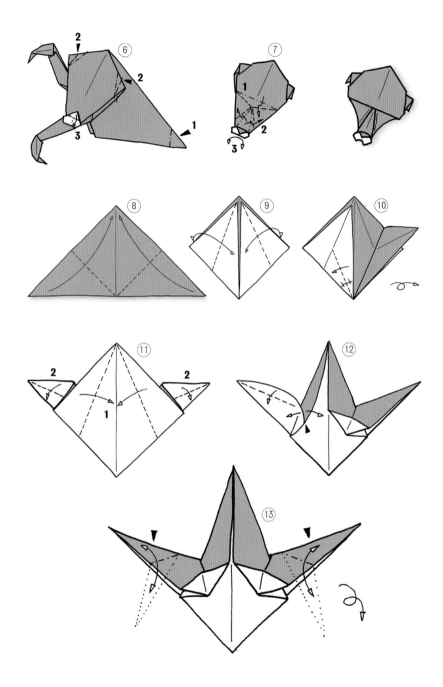

14 **Fold** the upper triangle (**1**) and mark the lower square (**2**). Perform the steps before folding everything in half along the vertical axis.

Details for making the leg

14a **Lift up** the tip.

14b **Mark** the creases as on the right.

14c **Push in** the creases using reverse folds as on the right.

15 **Cut out** the tail (**1**), then open everything (**2**).

16 **Release** the tail, then fold the lower square in half, encasing the left part between the layers of the right part. Everything is refolded automatically in half to give volume.

17 **To make the feet**, make inside reverse folds after pre-creasing.

Detail for assembly

18 **Slip** the lozenge of the lower part (**1**) between the central layers of the upper part (**2**). Slip the reverse fold of the upper piece (**3**) into the groove of the lower piece (**4**).

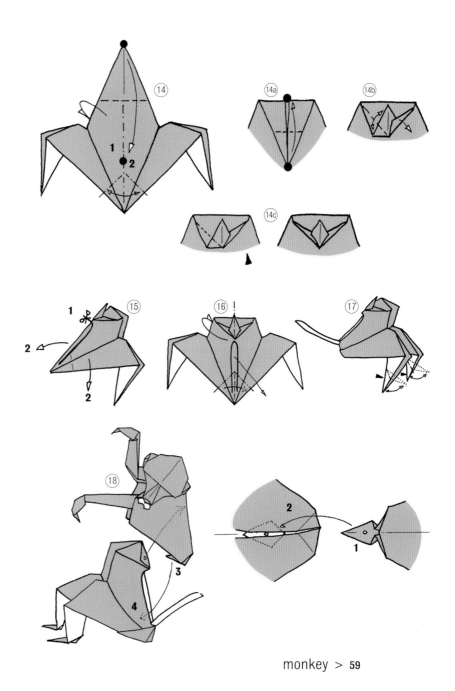

Fun and functional

Jet plane

This Japanese model is a paper plane that, when launched, will return to its starting point, making a large loop.

For recommended paper, see pp. 189 and 192

1. **Fold** the sides into the pre-marked centre.

2. **Turn** over.

3. **Join** the dots, which can be seen against the light.

4. **Fold down** the sides.

5. **Lift up** the tip.

6. **Join** the sides to the centre.

7. **Fold** in half behind.

8. **Place** the wings vertically. Hold at the point indicated to launch it with a straight arm.

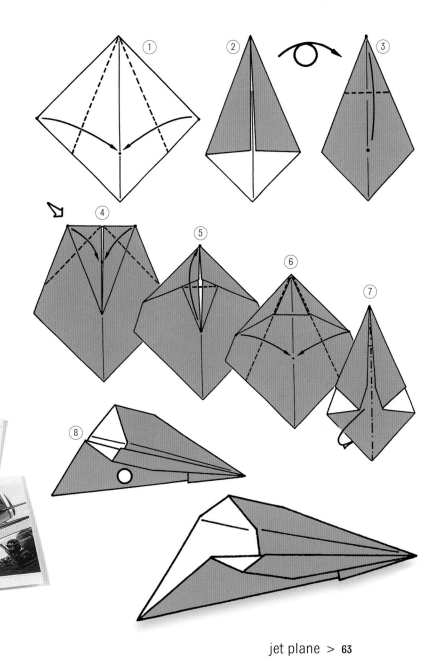

jet plane > **63**

Aeroplane

Due to its wide wings, this model has a <u>stable</u>, very slow flight. It is remarkably easy to make too.

For recommended paper, see pp. 193 and 196

1. **Mark** the vertical axis, then fold down the angles.

2. **Fold** the tips to the dot.

3. **Fold** the angles in half, then pinch the tip.

4. **Fold down** the tip to the left, then turn over.

5. **Join up** at the centre.

6. **To form the aerofoils**, mark the sides joining the dots, then fold in half behind.

7. **Fold down** the wings towards the outside.

8. **Hold** underneath and throw.

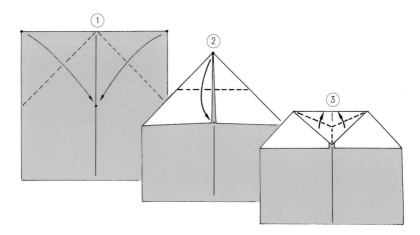

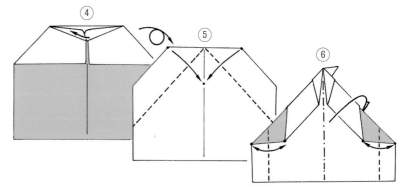

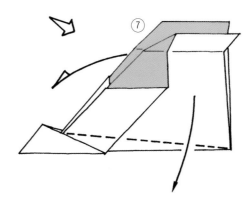

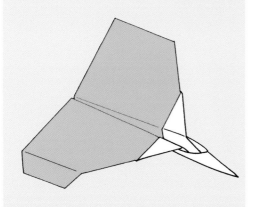

Fighter plane

Made from starry paper, this traditional Japanese model has aerofoils that give it good flight stability.

For recommended paper, see pp. 197 and 200

1. **Fold down** the tips towards the centre, pre-creased.
2. **Join** the marked dots.
3. **Fold down** the sides again.
4. **Turn** over.
5. **Fold** in half.
6. **Fold down** one side to the outside.
7. **Lift** the aerofoils and fold the other side behind.
8. **Angle** the wings upwards. Hold the plane underneath to launch.

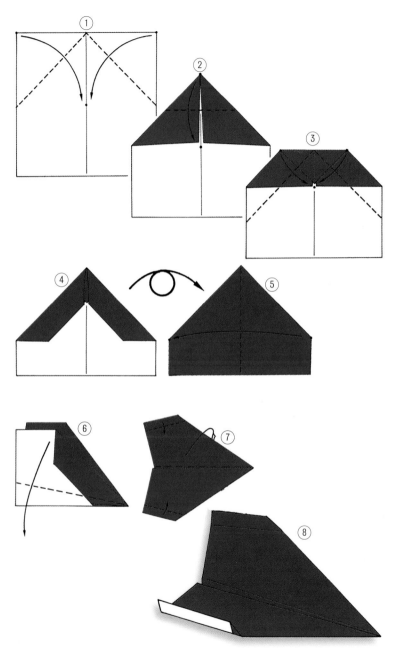

fighter plane > **67**

Concord

Although it looks like a dart, the Concord has a nose that is reinforced with several thicknesses of paper, enabling it to fly long distances without coming apart.

For recommended paper, see pp. 201 and 204

1. **Mark** the central vertical crease, then fold a quarter of the sheet into the centre.

2. **Mark** the creases by turning down the corners into the centre, then unfold.

3. **Place** the creases in the right direction, then reflatten.

4. **Lift up** each side.

5. **Slip** the tips under the first layer.

6. **Fold** the sides into the centre.

7. **Fold** in half behind.

8. **Adjust** the wings. To launch the plane, hold at the point indicated.

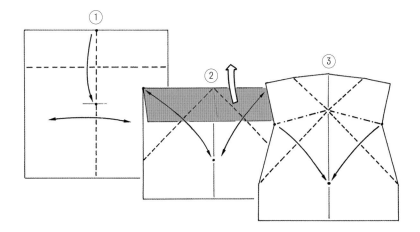

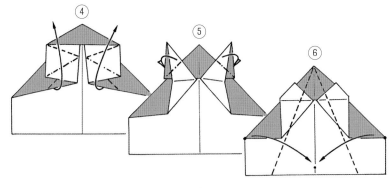

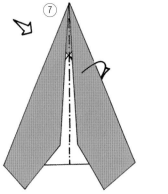

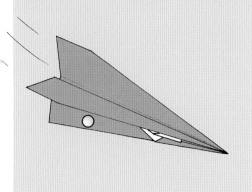

concord > **69**

Passenger aircraft

This model, folded from a paper reminiscent of holidays in the sun, can fly remarkably well.

For recommended paper, see pp. 205 and 208

1. **Fold** the tip to the right quarter without cutting into the centre crease.

2. **Fold down** the other side.

3. **Fold** the tip, then unfold everything.

4. **Place** the creases as indicated, then fold over the central tip.

5. **Insert** the sides into one another.

6. **Lift up** the tip.

7. **Fold** in half behind.

8. **Turn down** the edges, joining the dots.

Variation

8a. **Fold down** the edges, joining the dots, then fold down two stabilisers.

9. **Place** the wings slightly above the horizontal.

To launch the plane hold it underneath.

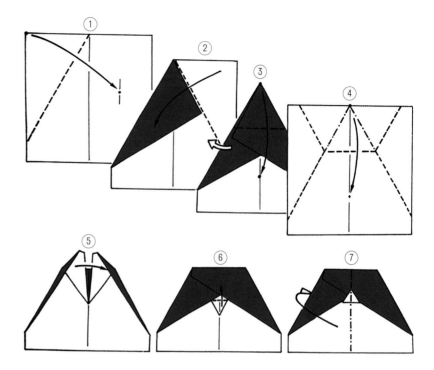

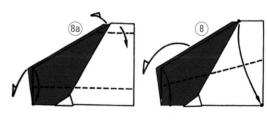

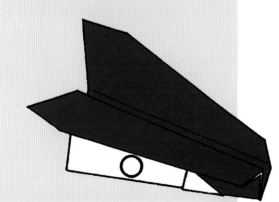

passenger aircraft > 71

Cube

These cubes, more commonly known as water bombs, are perfect for juggling. They have been made in brightly coloured 'snake' paper for an eyecatching effect.

For recommended paper, see pp. 209 and 212

1. **Mark** the horizontal crease.
2. **Mark** the vertical crease.
3. **Mark** the first diagonal in mountain fold (see p. 10).
4. **Mark** the second in the same way.
5. **Check** your model is as shown.
6. **Take** the square in both hands, sink the sides and squash.
7. **Check** you have a triangle as shown.
8. **Lift up** the sides.
9. **Fold down** the sides to the centre.
10. **Fold over** the upper tips.
11. **Slip** the triangles into the side pockets.
12. **Check** your model is as shown, then turn over.
13. **Repeat** steps 8 to 12 on the other face.
14. **To give it volume**, blow hard into the end.

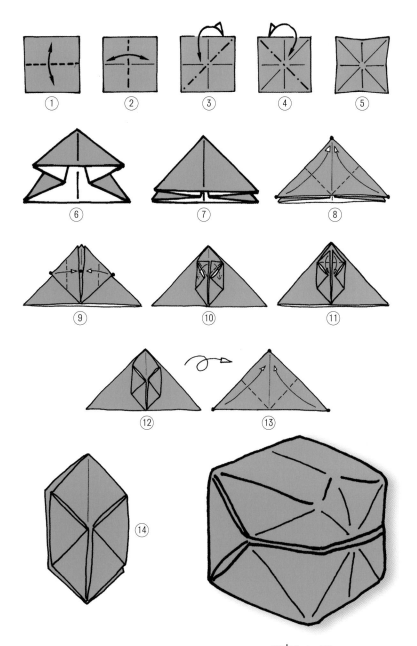

cube > **73**

Talking mouth

This pretty talking mouth is simply folded from 'strawberry' paper – all that is missing is some speech!

For recommended paper, see pp. 213 and 216

1. **Mark** the horizontal crease, then fold it in half towards the right.

2. **Mark** the creases by joining the sides together along the centre crease.

3. **Fold** the four corners, then unfold the corners of the right side.

4. **Fold** along the outside edge on the left side. On the right side, fold the first layer along the marked crease, then repeat behind.

5. **Unfold** the left corners, then open the paper.

6. **Fold over** the sides along the centre crease.

7. **Mark** the crease at the four corners along the top layer.

8. **Fold down** the corners making an inside reverse fold (see p. 11).

9. **Reverse** the narrow strips to finish off the sides, by folding them inside, beneath the layers.

10. **To form the mouth**, lift the triangles as indicated then fold in half.

11. **Turn in** the edges.

   To make the mouth talk, hold the folded paper at the marked dots, then gently move your hands together and apart.

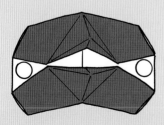

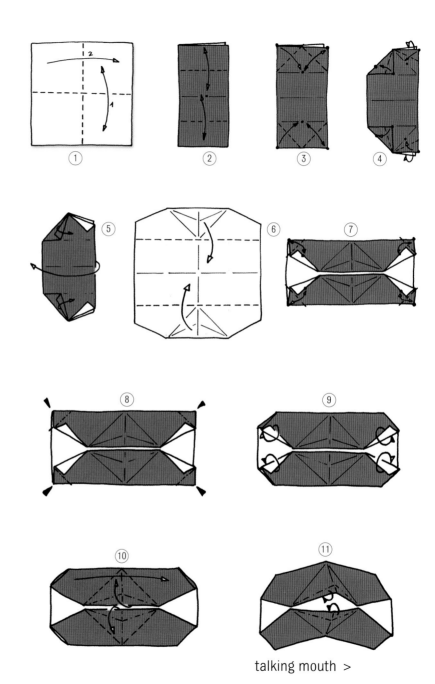

talking mouth >

Open box

This elegant box, made from 'crumpled' paper, is ideal for holding pot pourri, sweets, pencils and other little treats.

For recommended paper, see pp. 217 and 220

1. **Mark** the vertical crease and the horizontal crease, unfold.

2. **Fold** in half, joining the dots.

3. **Mark** the creases by turning down the sides to the centre.

4. **Fold down** the left side, joining the dots.

5. **Fold** the two corners.

6. **Fold down** the side towards the left.

7. **Fold down** the right side, joining the dots.

8. **Fold** the two corners then fold over towards the right.

9. **Open** by pressing on the sides.

10. **Flatten** by joining the dots.

11. **Pinch** the sides to give the box volume.

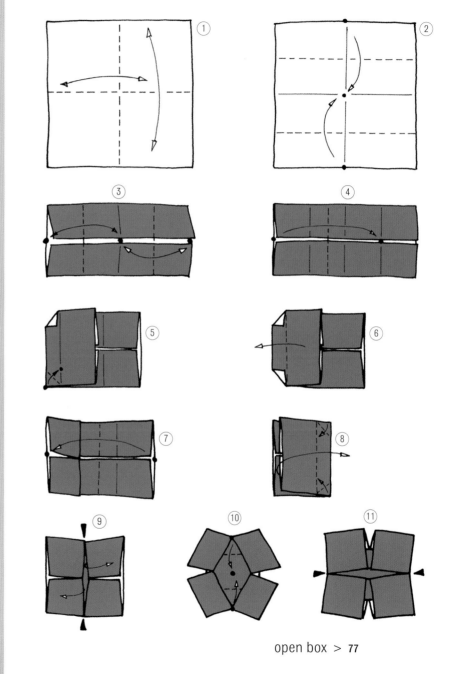

open box > 77

Packet

Filled with peanuts, this packet has an amazing visual effect. Make it from a range of different papers and fill it with whatever you wish.

For recommended paper, see pp. 221 and 224

1. **Mark** the diagonals.

2. **Fold** the angle in half without marking the end.

3. **Fold down** the tip along the diagonal, just marking the inside fold, then unfold.

4. **Repeat** steps 2 and 3 for the three other sides, then fold each side as shown in step 3.

5. **Place** the tips on the inside.

6. **Mark** the bottom as a square to obtain the packet shape.

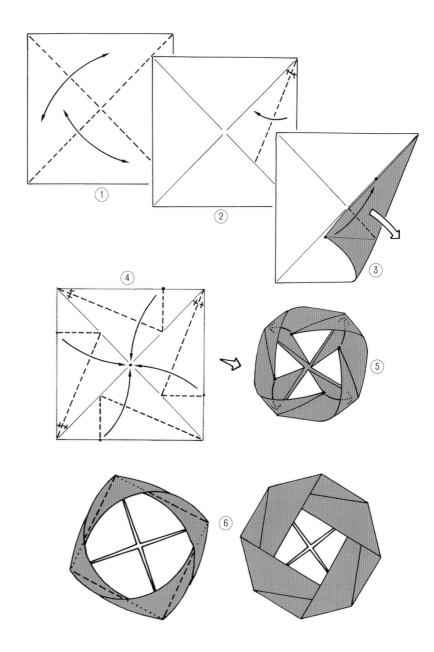

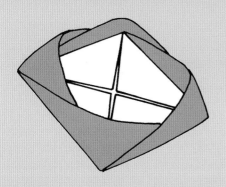

Dish

With its elegant lines, this dish looks stunning when made from a green wood effect paper. You can vary the papers used to achieve a different effect.

For recommended paper, see pp. 225 and 228

1. **Pinch** the diagonals to find the centre, then join the four corners at the central point.

2. **Check** your model is as shown, then turn over.

3. **Fold** to the centre releasing the tips at the back.

4. **Reposition** the tips behind.

5. **Fold** the two other sides to the centre, releasing the tips behind.

6. **Check** your model is as shown, then open completely.

7. **Mark** the creases.

8. **Give** it volume, then see the detail.

9. **Fold** the square and the triangle, joining the dots.

10. **Sink** the right part before pushing in the narrow strip.

11. **Check** your model is as shown, then repeat on the three other sides.

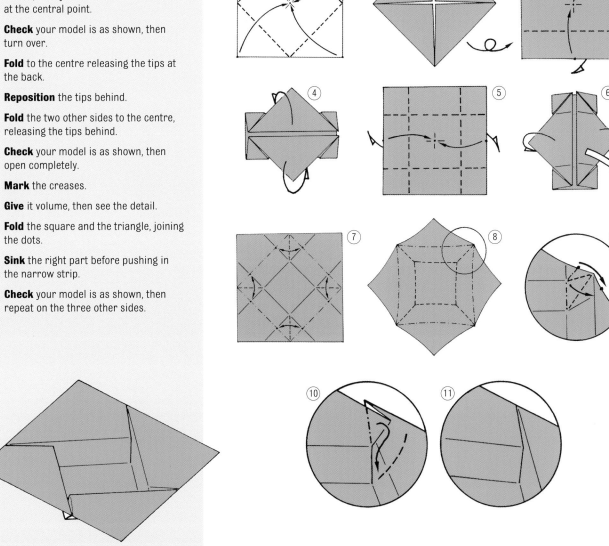

Spiral

When this model is thrown from a certain height, it turns faster and faster due to its curved blades that slice through the air as it falls.

For recommended paper, see pp. 229 and 232

1. **Join** the tips in pairs to mark the creases, then turn over.

2. **Mark** the creases by folding in half, then turn over.

3. **Join** the four tips.

4. **Check** your model is as shown.

5. **Mark** the two sides, then repeat behind.

6. **Open** completely in the opposite direction.

7. **Place** the creases in the right direction.

8. **Mark** the sides by matching up the edges.

9. **Fold** each side by turning underneath inside. When the last side is folded, the model is under tension.

10. **The spiral should turn** as it falls. If not, place it on to a thin stick then blow.

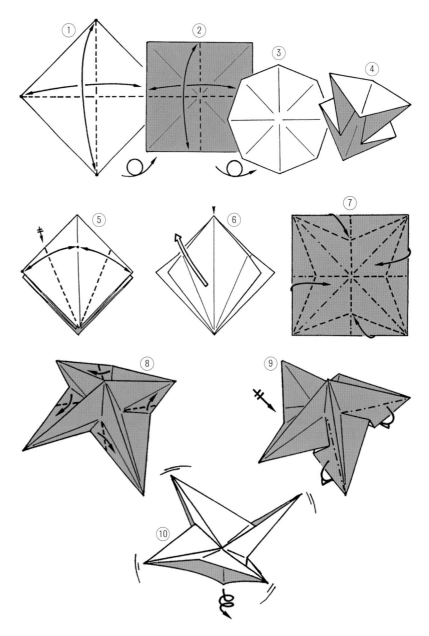

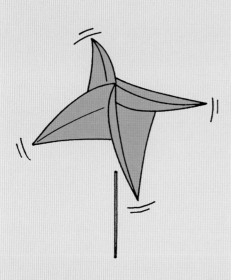

Frisbee

As it is so light, this frisbee can only be used indoors. Have fun making it in a combination of different papers for a brightly coloured effect.

For recommended paper, see pp. 233 to 264. Use eight squares of paper

1. **Fold** the square in half as indicated.

2. **Mark** the right side by folding the angle in half onto one layer.

3. **Fold down** the tip onto the dot.

4. **Mark** all the layers.

5. **Unfold** the tip, then push it inside by opening slightly (see p. 11 inside reverse fold).

6. **Mark** the halfway point as indicated, then fold down one tip.

7. **Fold** eight of them in total. Fit each one into the other by its tip.

8. **Once the tip has been placed inside**, fold down the triangles inside in front and behind to fit everything together firmly.

9. **Check** your model is as shown.

10. **Once the crown is finished,** mark a light border, then turn everything over. The frisbee is ready to be thrown.

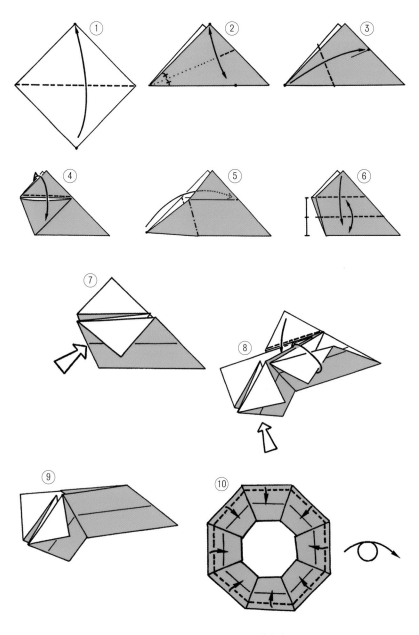

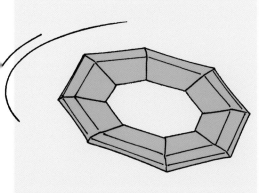

frisbee > 85

Fighter squadron

This plane is a traditional Chinese model. Assembling several little planes on a larger one gives a powerful finishing touch.

For recommended paper, see pp. 265, 268, 269 and 272. Use two squares of paper

1. **Mark** the centre in both directions.

2. **Mark** the diagonals on opposite creases. Gather up the half-diagonals two by two.

3. **Lift up** the tips.

4. **Bring** the sides to the centre.

5. **Bend** the tip behind.

6. **Turn** over.

7. **Bring** the two dots to the centre.

8. **Roll** a tight rectangle in the same paper between one third and two thirds of the size of the initial square.

9. **Slip** the stick between the two layers underneath, then fold down the sides under the tip.

10. **Pull** the inside tips as far apart as possible.

11. **Fold** the aerofoils. Place the other smaller planes under the wings.

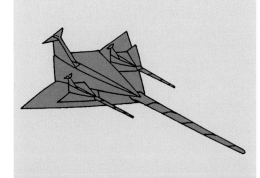

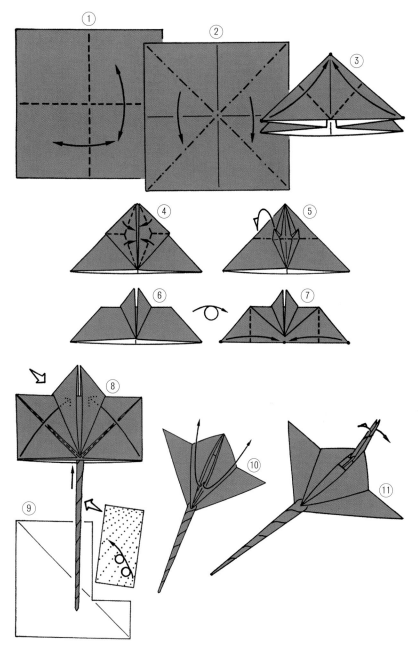

fighter squadron > 87

Bookmark

Take this little lotus flower with you whenever you're reading. For a modern look, this bookmark is made from 'patchwork magazine' paper.

For recommended paper, see pp. 273 and 276

1. **Mark** the diagonals in mountain fold (see p. 10).

2. **Mark** the centre in valley fold (see p. 10), then give some volume to the water bomb base (see p. 12).

3. **Lift up** the tips at the dots indicated.

4. **Lift up** the two other tips, spacing them apart.

5. **Check** your model is as shown, then unfold completely.

6. **Place** the upper triangles inside the lower ones.

7. **Fold down** the four tips behind, then put back into their creases.

8. **Slip** the bookmark over the corner of a page in your book.

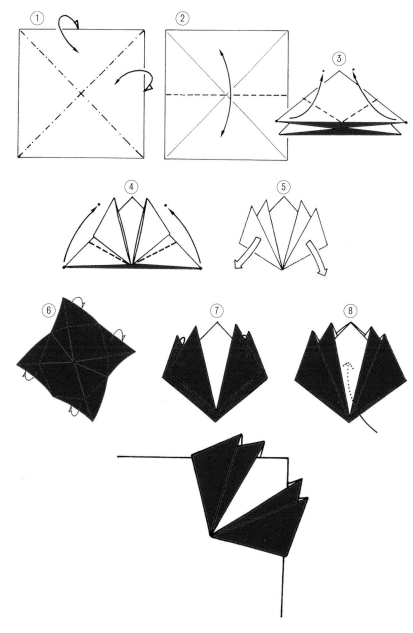

Photo frame

This stylish little patchwork frame is ready to receive a photo of your loved ones or your holiday memories.

For recommended paper, see pp. 277, 280, 281 and 284. Use two squares of paper

1. **Mark** the centre of the square with a slight crease on the four sides.

2. **Take** another square and lightly mark its four corners with a crease.

3. **Place** the square marked at the corners beneath the other square, matching up their creases. Fold down the four corners of the underneath square onto the top square.

4. **Fold down** the upper and lower strips joining the dots as indicated.

5. **Mark** the two side strips with a crease, joining the dots. Unfold, then refold slipping the corners under the first layer.

6. **Slip** a photo inside the frame.

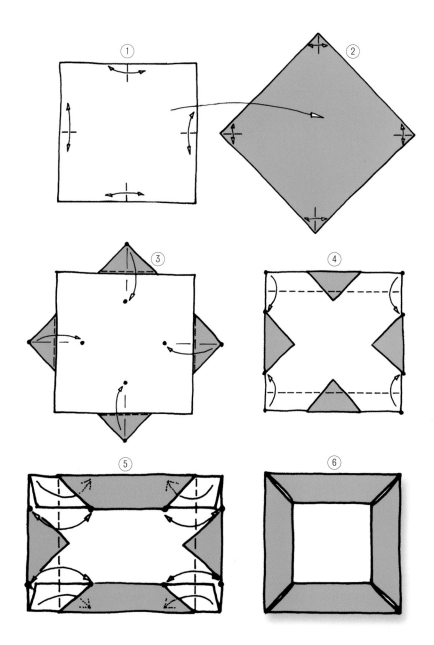

Wings and feathers

Owl

As suggested by this paper, the owl is a nocturnal bird with striking plumage that lives in the hollows of trees.

For recommended paper, see pp. 285 and 288

1. **Fold** a square in half, joining the dots.

2. **Fold** the left side, then the right side joining the dots on the horizontal.

3. **Fold down** one side towards the right.

4. **Fold down** the other towards the left.

5. **Hold** onto one point with your hand and lift up each tip by slipping your thumb inside to make the pleat.

6. **Check** your model is as shown, then turn the piece over.

7. **Fold** the top part downwards.

8. **Starting at the centre**, fold over a triangle from each side.

9. **Make** a pleat to form the beak.

10. **Shape the eyes** by slipping the end of your finger into the two long folds behind the beak, then fold the sides and the bottom inside.

   To make the owl stand upright, slightly open the base and bend the wings.

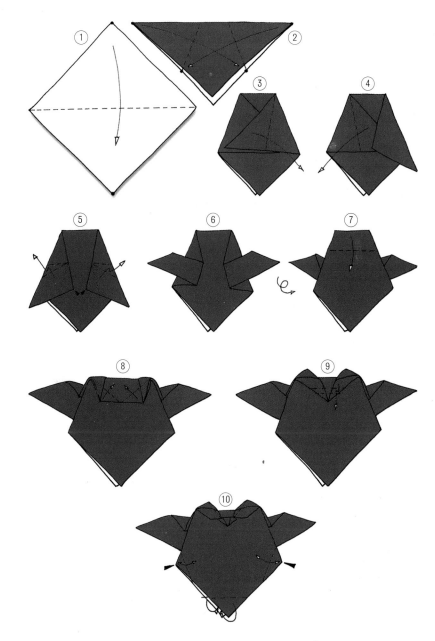

Butterfly

This beautiful little butterfly is folded from paper decorated with *farfalle* pasta (which means butterfly in Italian).

For recommended paper, see pp. 289 and 292

1. **Fold** a square of paper in half.

2. **Fold** in half again.

3. **To make the antennae**, cut the edge through all the layers.

4. **Lift up** one layer, joining the dots.

5. **Make** a pleat by folding the triangle downwards.

6. **Lift up** to the top joining the dots.

7. **Cut** along the unbroken line, then turn the piece over.

8. **Fold** in half.

9. **Cut** along the unbroken lines through all the layers.

10. **Fold** the first wing at an angle.

11. **Check** your model is as shown, then turn the piece over.

12. **Fold** the other wing, joining the dots.

13. **Open** the butterfly and adjust the antennae.

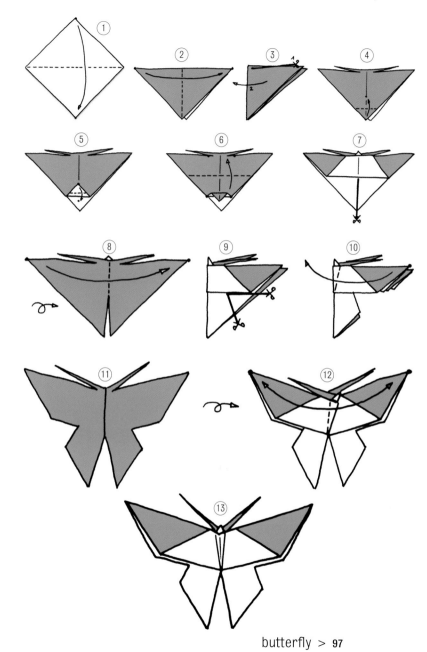

butterfly > **97**

Parrot

A brightly coloured parrot that can be made to stand on its perch by folding over the ends of its claws. To make this parrot, start with the bird base, of course...

For recommended paper, see pp. 293 and 296

1. **Prepare** a bird base (see p. 14). Lift up a tip onto each face.

2. **Turn** a flap onto each face.

3. **Cut** through all the layers along the unbroken line, then turn the flaps as in the previous step.

4. **Pre-crease** the two lower tips by folding them along the horizontal. Lift up the left one to the vertical, then press on the centre crease to make a squash fold.

5. **Mark** the creases, then push in the sides in a reverse fold.

Details for the feet

5a. **Bend** the tip towards the left, then repeat the previous steps for the right tip.

6. **Fold** the tips in half.

7. **Open** the central part. Fold the tips downwards, folding them between the layers as on the right.

8. **To make the feet**, make reverse folds after pre-creasing, then turn everything over.

9. **Fold** one tip downwards.

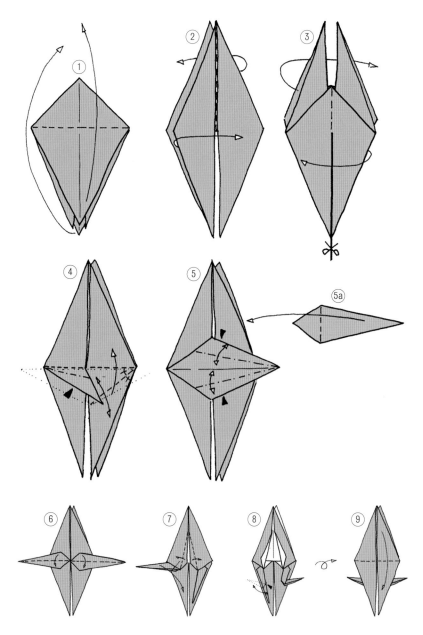

parrot > 99

Parrot (cont.)

10 **Lift up** the tip, joining the dots.

11 **Fold** the two tips downwards together.

12 **Fold** in half towards the back.

13 **To make the head**, make an outside reverse fold (see p. 11) after pre-creasing. For the feet, fold an inside reverse fold (see p. 11).

Details for the head

13a **Make** a pre-crease for the beak, then fold the tip downwards holding it at the point indicated.

13b **Pre-crease** the beak again (**1**). Push the angle into a reverse fold (**2**). Make a reverse fold at the tip of the cheeks after pre-creasing (**3**). Give shape to the forehead.

13c **Finish** the beak with an outside reverse fold (see p. 11).

Details for the feet

13d **Fold over** the end of the feet in a reverse fold, so that the bird can hold onto its perch.

14 **Push in** the sides.

Add the finishing touches, by shaping the head and bending the wings.

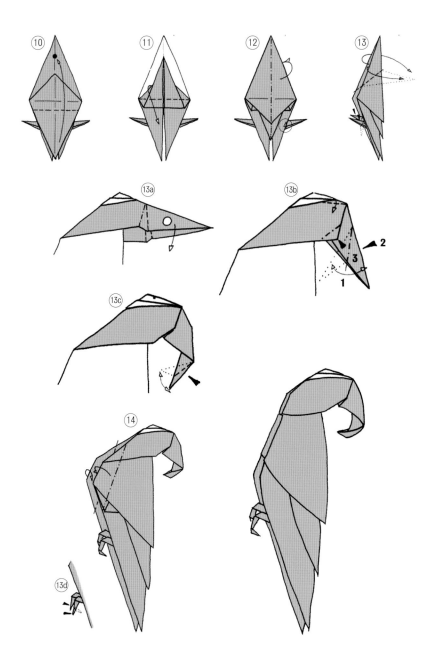

Grasshopper

This insect, found in the fields in summer, can jump
surprisingly high using its long, hind legs.

For recommended paper,
see pp. 297 and 300

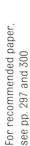

Grasshopper (cont.)

1 **Fold** in half.

2 **Lift up** the sides on each face, leaving a space at the upper edge.

3 **Fold** the sides in half again on each face.

4 **Cut** a fine opening through all the layers.

5 **To make the antennae**, fold forward the strip in each opening as far as possible.

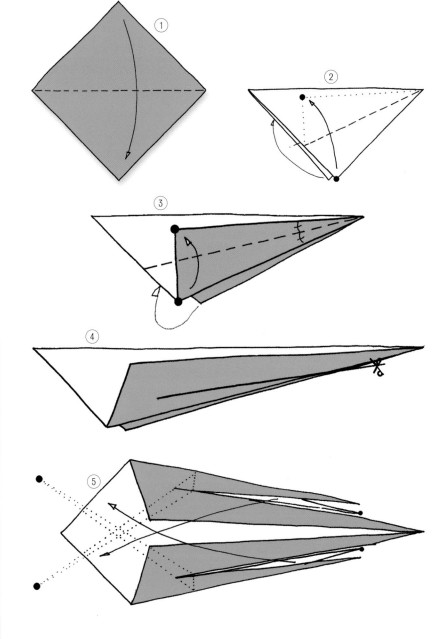

6 Fold the two other strips in an inside reverse fold (see p. 11) after pre-creasing. On the left part, fold down the sides towards the centre; on the rear right part, make a series of pleats.

7 Fold everything in half.

8 Make a reverse fold by folding the antennae on the front left part. Fold the feet in a reverse fold.

Detail for the head

8a Lift up the antennae and the head.

Detail for the legs

8b Make a reverse fold at the ends of the legs.

To finish, shape the body by rounding.

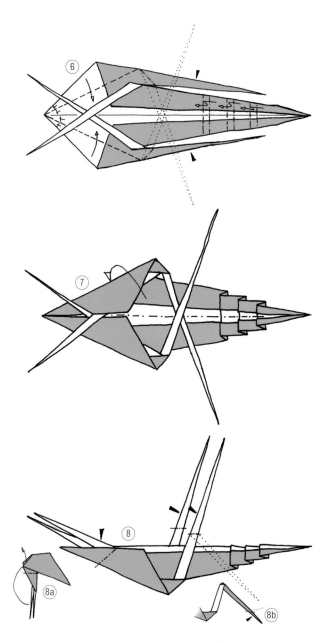

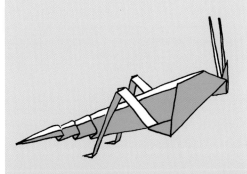

grasshopper > 103

Dove

This symbol of peace can be suspended by attaching a length of fishing line to each of its wings. Hanging several together will give the stunning impression of birds in flight.

For recommended paper, see pp. 301 and 304

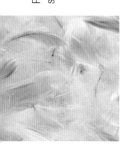

1. **Take** half a square and make a pre-crease by turning down the sides onto the centre vertical crease (**1**). Mark the creases for the base, joining the dots (**2**).

2. **Mark** this crease by folding down each tip onto the opposite side, joining the dots located on the horizontal.

2a. **Check** your model is as shown, then unfold.

3. **Reverse** the previous creases, then join the dots.

4. **Fold down** the tips onto the horizontal line, flattening the creases inside.

5. **Mark** the crease of the upper tip, then open this tip.

Details for the rear

5a. **Push** the tip inside by reversing the creases, then turn the piece over.

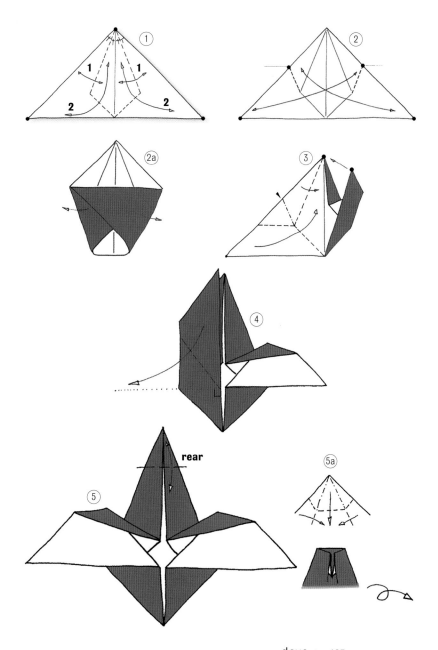

dove > 105

Dove (cont.)

6 **Fold** the lower edges (**1**) then fold the upper edges to slim down the body (**2**).

7 **Fold** in half.

8 **Make** an outside reverse fold (see p. 11) at the front and the rear.

9 **Make** a pleat at the tip of the head. To curve the wings, make a series of pleats.

Details

9a **At the front**, push the corner into a reverse fold.

9b **At the rear**, make a triangle by pressing at the centre to give volume.

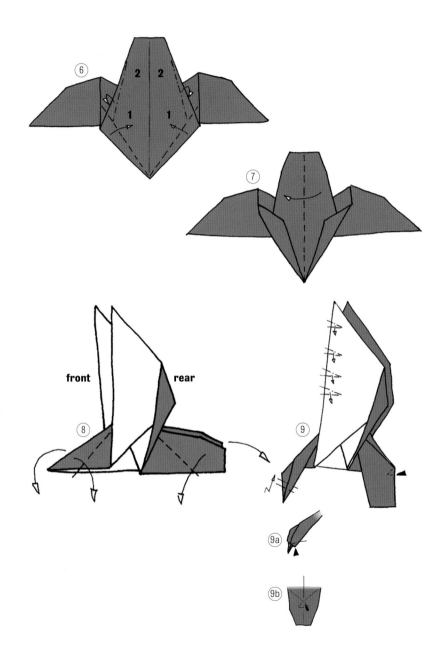

Bird

This bird is positioned ready to fly away to her nest. You can also make a bird that is standing at rest, like the sparrows that you find on window ledges.

For recommended paper, see pp. 305 and 308

Bird (cont.)

1 **Make** the bird base (see p. 14) and fold down the two sides.

2 **Turn** one flap onto each face.

3 **Fold** each tip horizontally, in a reverse fold.

Bird at rest

4 **Start with the legs**: reduce the tips by folding them in half (**1**) then make a reverse fold for each one (**2**). Continue folding the legs following steps 4a and 4b. Next, cut the upper tip in half and fold the two parts downwards (**3**). Fold everything in half, towards the back, along the centre crease (**4**).

Details

4a **Make** a pleat lifting the tips again.

4b **Check** your model is as shown.

5 **Fold over** the wings towards the back (**1**). Fold over the tips of the feet (see p. 15). Make a reverse fold for the head (**2**).

5a **Fold** the wings downwards.

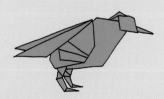

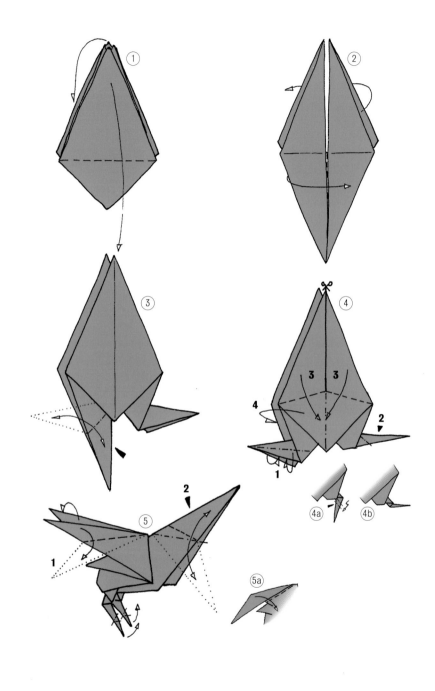

Details for the head

5b **Lift up** the tip in a reverse fold.

5c **Fold** the tip downwards opening the sides.

5d **Hold** the dot between the thumb and index finger, then bend the tip downwards.

5e **Make** a pleat for the beak in a reverse fold (see p. 15).

5f **Slim down** the tip of the beak by folding the sides underneath.

Bird in flight

4 **To make the bird with its wings spread**, cut the first tip in half then fold the wings (**1**). Fold over behind along the vertical axis (**2**).

Details

4a **Open** each tip (**1**) and lift it up vertically (**2**).

4b **Fold down** one side.

4c **Push in** the base, then make a series of pleats to curve the wings.

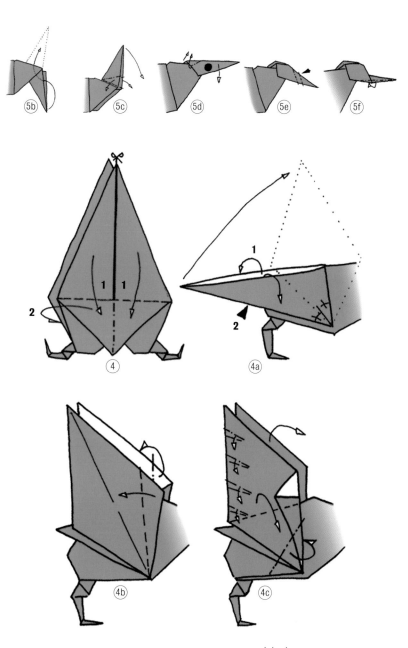

Hen

This home-loving hen has slipped into an attractive checked costume. The print immediately brings to mind the style of a traditional kitchen.

For recommended paper, see pp. 309 and 312

1 **Start** with the fish base (see p. 16). Fold down the two lower sides of the lozenge along the centre crease and mark the crease. Fold over the two little flaps along the centre crease and mark the crease. Open by folding in half the lower edges and lifting the tips towards the outside.

2 **Reduce** the width of the side tips by folding them in half again.

3 **Bend** the side tips towards the back and downwards around the axis of the dotted line (**1**). Mark the two horizontal creases (**2**).

3a **Fold** the tips in half.

3b **Open** the top side tip (**1**) bending it to the centre (**2**).

3c **Mark** the horizontal crease.

4 **Mark** the horizontal creases using mountain folds (see p. 10) and the other creases of the triangle using valley folds (see p. 10), then turn over.

5 **Lift up** the two ends along the horizontal creases (**1**), giving shape to the two other sides of the triangles in mountain folds. Fold in half behind, along the centre crease (**2**).

6 **Make** a series of pleats for the tail. For the head, make a reverse fold after pre-creasing.

6a **Lift up** the tip in the same way.

6b **Lower** the tip to make the beak and the crest.

6c **Check** your model is as shown.

6d **Make** a reverse fold for the feet.

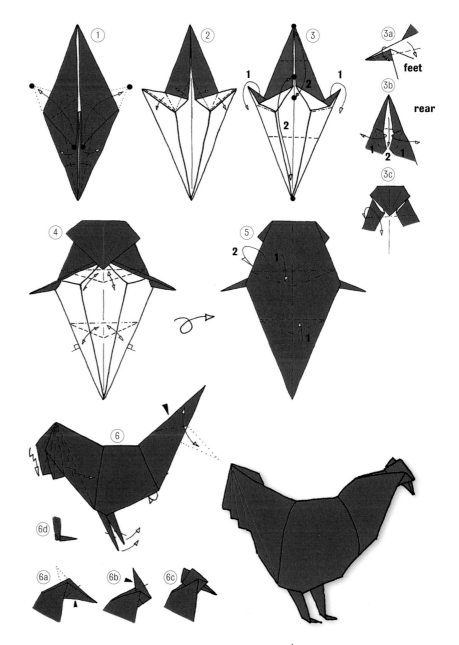

hen > 111

Chick

Which came first, the chicken or the egg? This age-old saying comes to mind when folding a chick that has just emerged from its shell...

For recommended paper, see pp. 313 and 316

1. **Fold** the square in half.
2. **Fold** towards the right.
3. **Fold** the upper tip towards the left.
4. **Lift** the tip upwards.
5. **Unfold** the tip.
6. **Make** a pleat on each side.
7. **Fold down** the tips on each side, joining the dots. To make the beak, make a pleat after pre-creasing.
7a. **Push** the triangle in a reverse fold on each face.
8. **Divide** the angle in half, then make a reverse fold on both faces.
9. **After pre-creasing** (**1**), fold the tips back between the layers (**2**) to put them back in the same place.

Details for the rear

10. **Block off** the rear by refolding the triangle inside.
10a. **Push** the rear in with a reverse fold. For the feet, make a pleat.

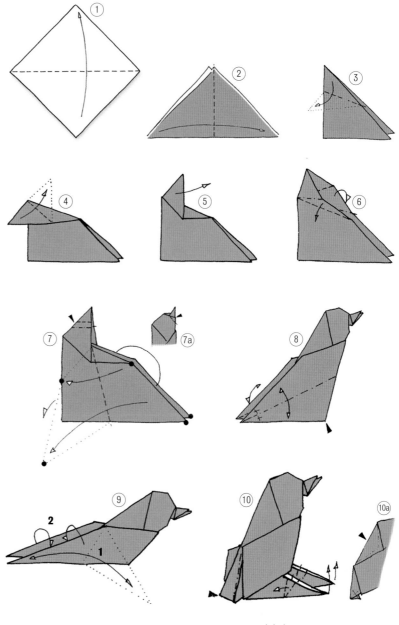

chick > 113

Heron

To make this heron stand up to show off its long beak and amazing plumage, slip a little piece of wire between the folds of its feet.

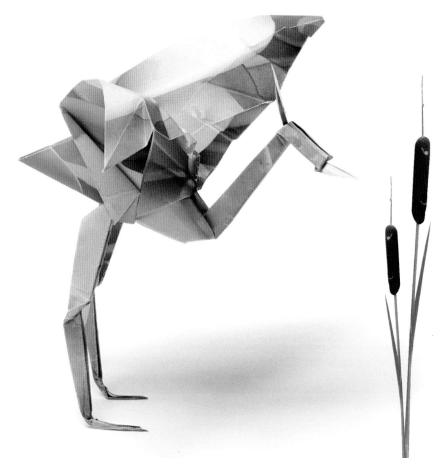

1 **Make** the bird base (see p. 14) and turn a flap to the right.

2 **Lift up** the whole tip horizontally by turning down the side towards the left.

3 **Turn** the flap to the left.

4 **Lift up** the tip horizontally in the same way by turning everything down towards the right.

5 **Fold** the sides from corner to corner.

6 **Lift up** the tip.

7 **Fold** the sides along the vertical, then turn over.

8 **Fold over** the sides along the centre crease.

9 **Fold** the sides of the tip, pinching the paper at the base of the wings, then under the body.

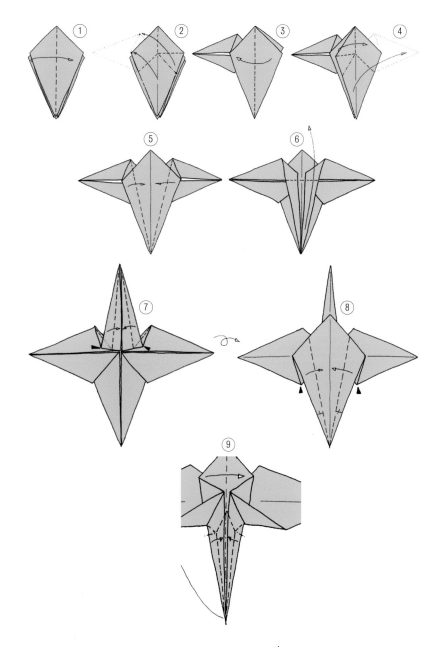

Heron (cont.)

10 **To make the head** on the right tip, mark off the portion for creasing. To make the legs, cut in half along the unbroken line then fold down the tips on each side.

Details for the head

10a **Open** the tip of the head and fold down the upper triangle (**1**). Fold the sides to the centre, then pinch at the base of the head to place the pleats flat (**2**).

10b **To make the crest**, cut a fine strip from each side, then make a pleat for the beak.

10c **Push** the corner into a reverse fold on each face.

Details for the legs

11 **Mark** the two creases at the centre of the legs, then make reverse folds and open.

To make the feet, fold ends of the legs horizontally (see p. 15).

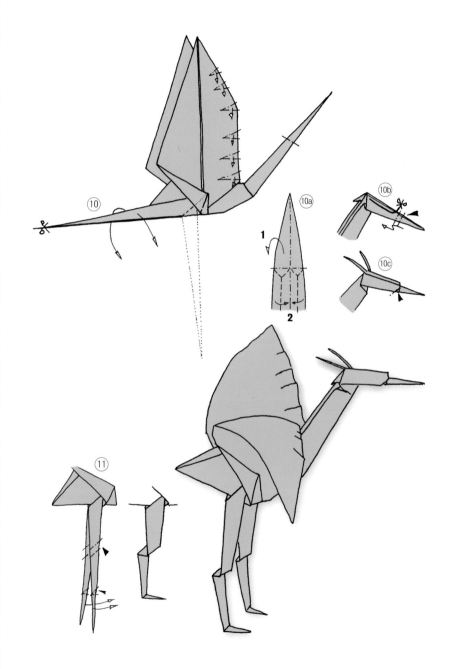

Eagle

This eagle with powerful outspread wings can carry a little object between its claws or can rest balancing on a branch to watch for its prey.

For recommended paper, see pp. 321 and 324

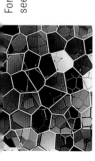

Eagle (cont.)

1 **Make the water bomb base** (see p.12) then fold down one tip onto each face along the centre crease and unfold.

2 **Make** a squash fold by opening the triangle in half on both sides.

3 **Mark** the creases by turning down the sides onto the centre crease, then push the sides in using reverse folds.

4 **Lift** the tip up, squashing everything, then turn over.

5 **Fold down** along the centre crease.

6 **Fold,** joining the dots.

7 **Fold down** the top of the wings, then slip the pleats between the layers of the central triangle.

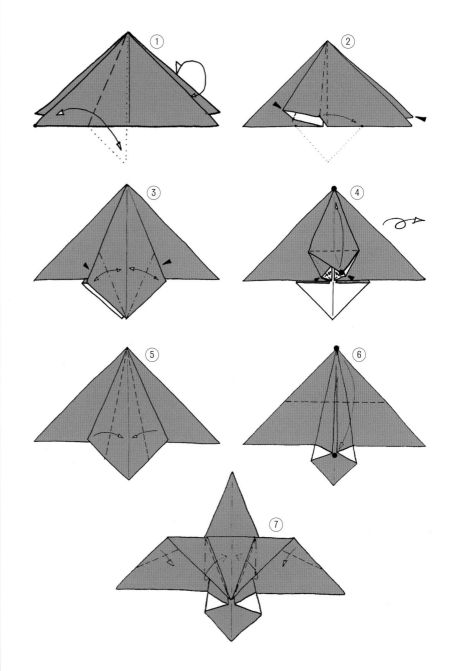

8 To make the feet, cut along the unbroken line through all the layers of the triangle. To make the head, fold down the upper tip towards the bottom.

Details for the head

8a Lift up the tip (**1**), then bend behind with a pleat (**2**).

8b Fold the sides, then turn over.

8c Lift up the triangle to form the beak.

8d Mark the creases as indicated, then turn over.

8e Make a pleat to give some volume.

8f To secure the pleat, push the triangle between the layers.

9 Fold down the upper sides underneath, fold over the excess located on the wings and fold everything in half.

10 Open the rear and shape using two creases. Fold the feet to the inside then finish the hooked beak with an inside reverse fold (see p. 11).

11 Slip the index finger or a little piece of wood between the eagle's feet.

Hey presto: it's ready to fly!

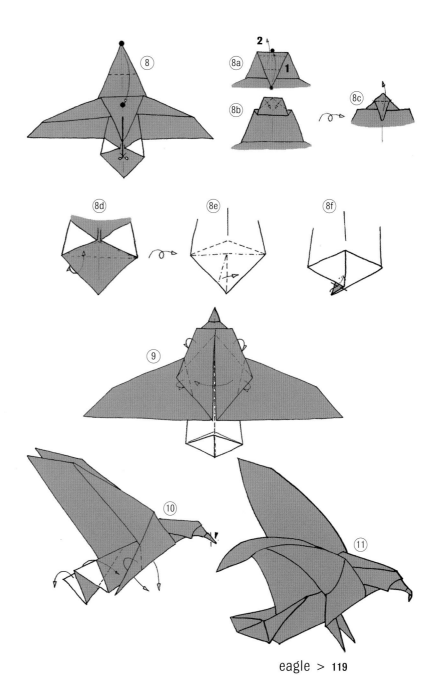

Papers

On the following pages, you will find a selection of papers that have been used to make the models in this book. Extra papers have also been supplied on pages 323–344 to enable you to let your imagination run riot and discover the wealth of expression available to you

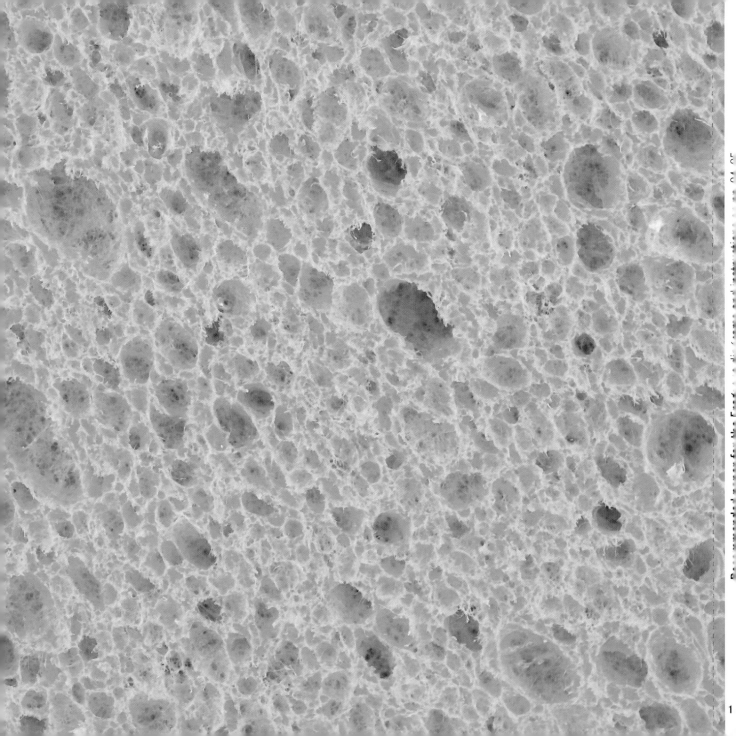

Recommended paper for the Rabbit: see diagrams and instructions on pp. 34, 35

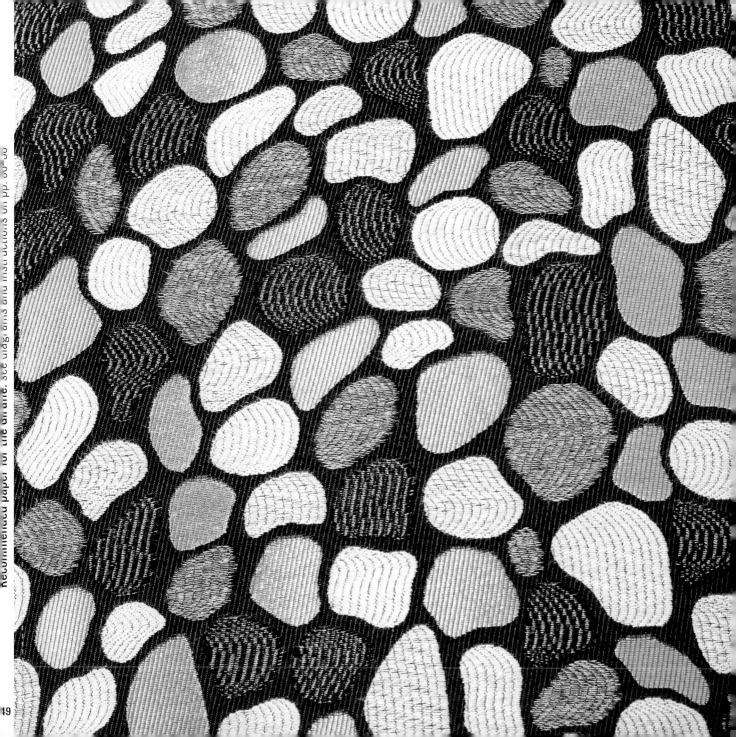

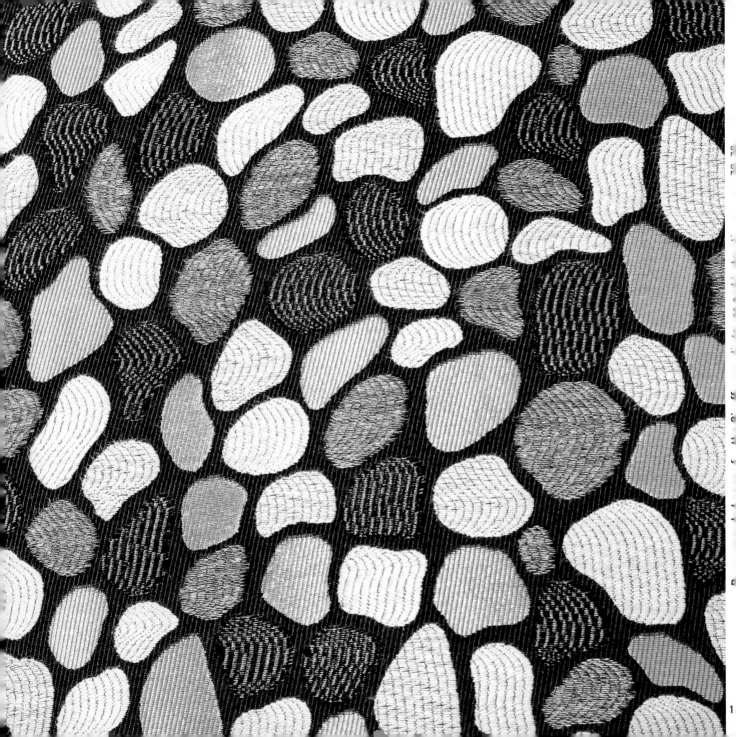

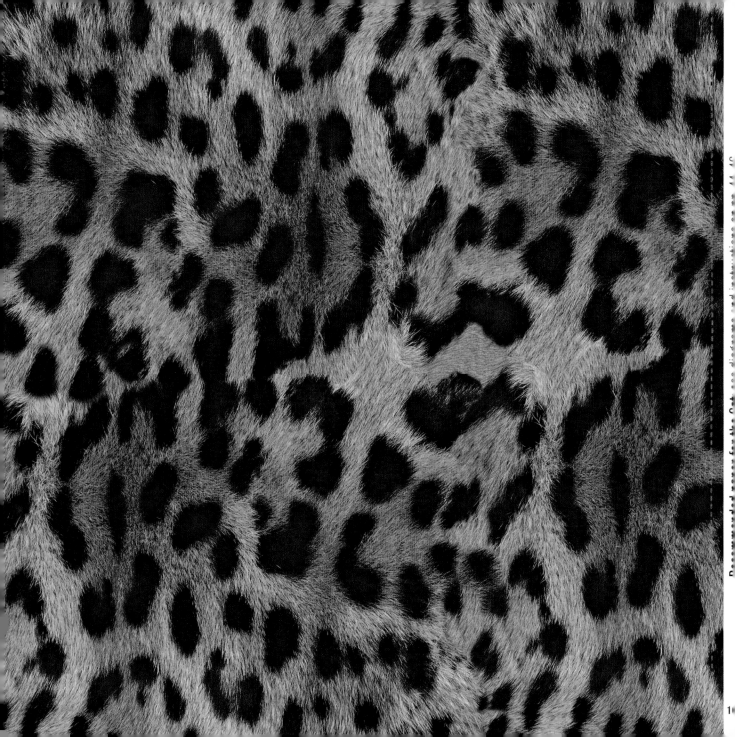

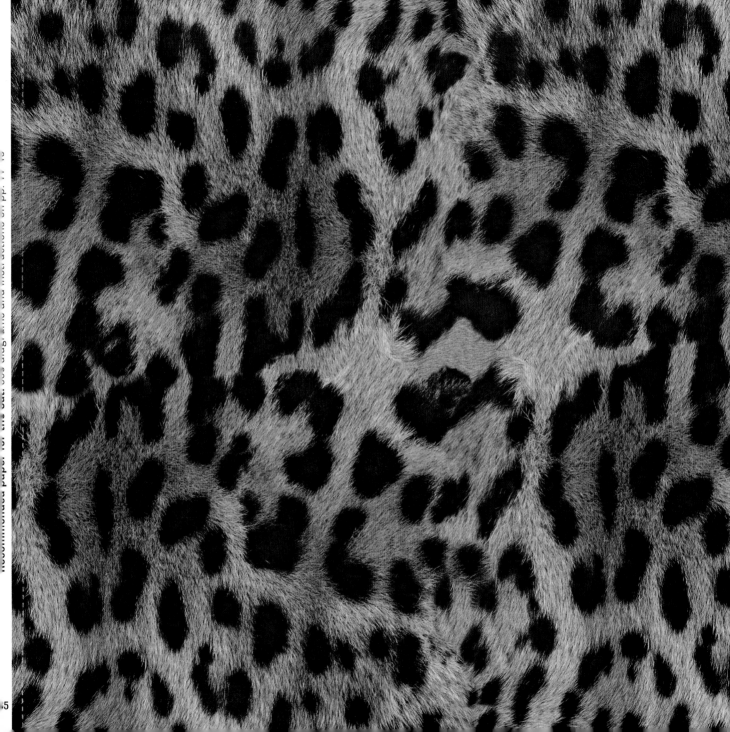

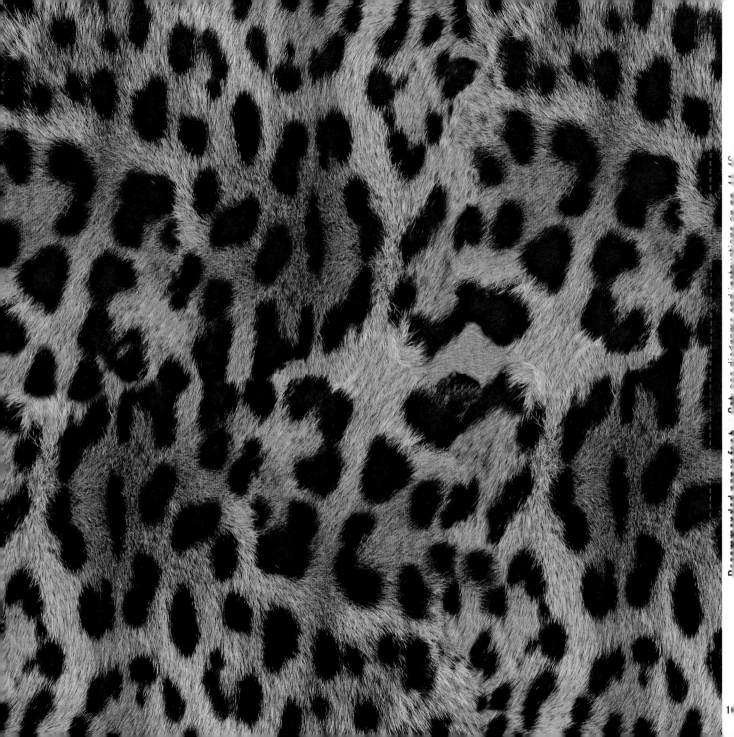

1

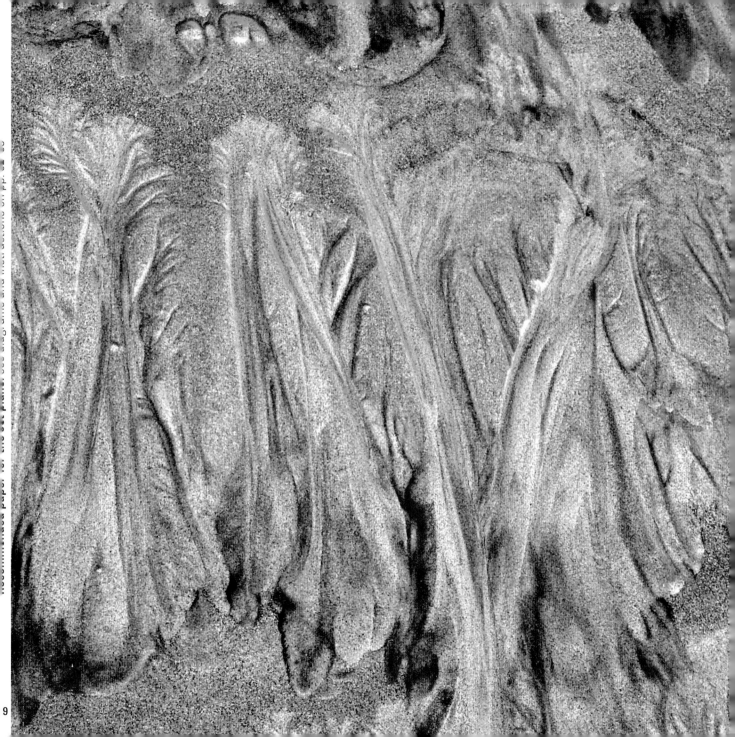

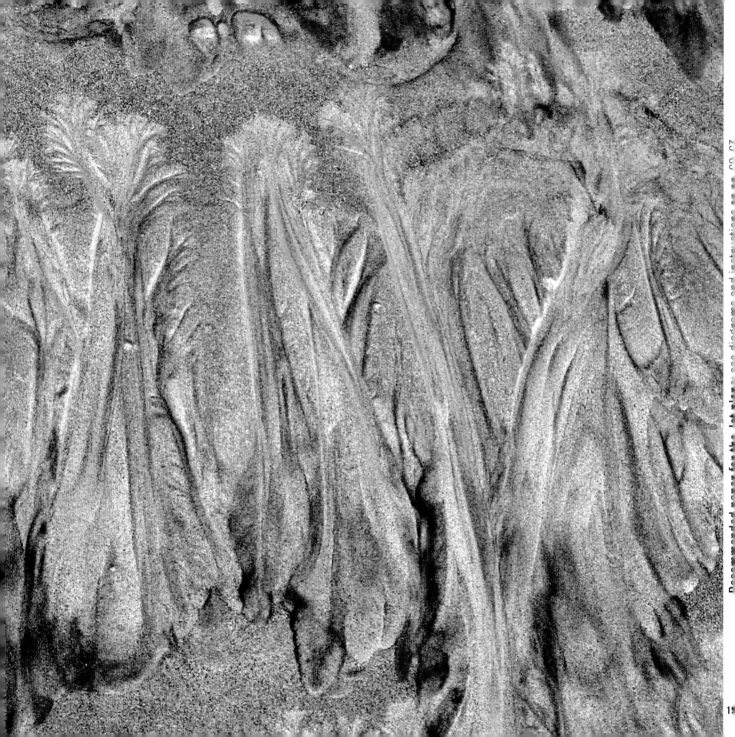

Recommended paper for the Packet: see diagrams and instructions on pp. 78-79

recommended paper for the Frisbee. See diagrams and instructions on pp. 64–66

1

3

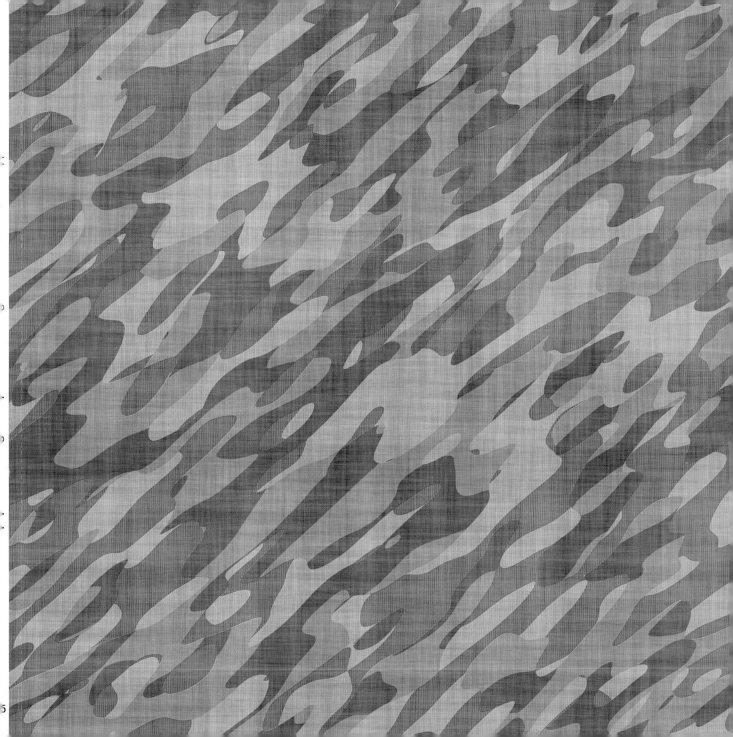

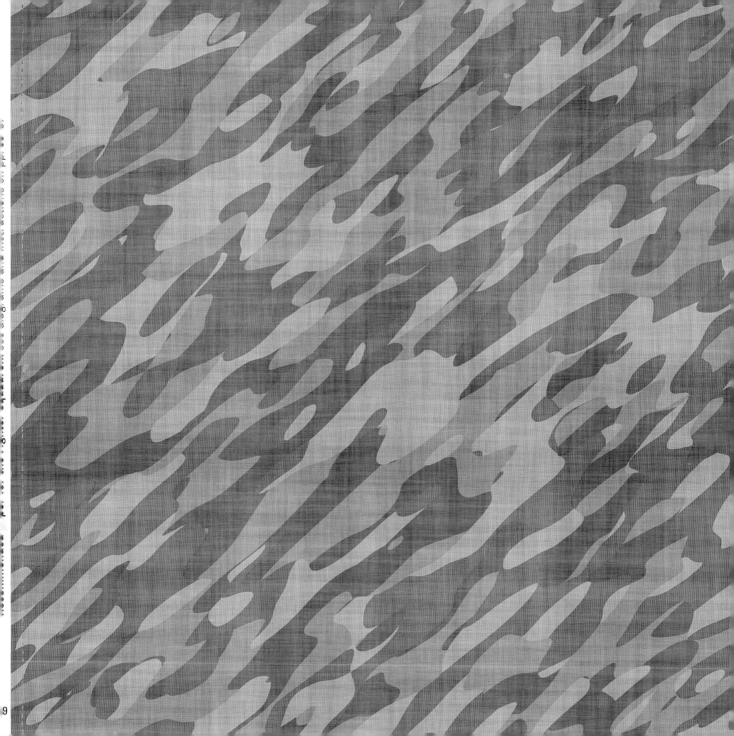

Recommended papers for the Dove; see diagrams and instructions on pp. 104–106

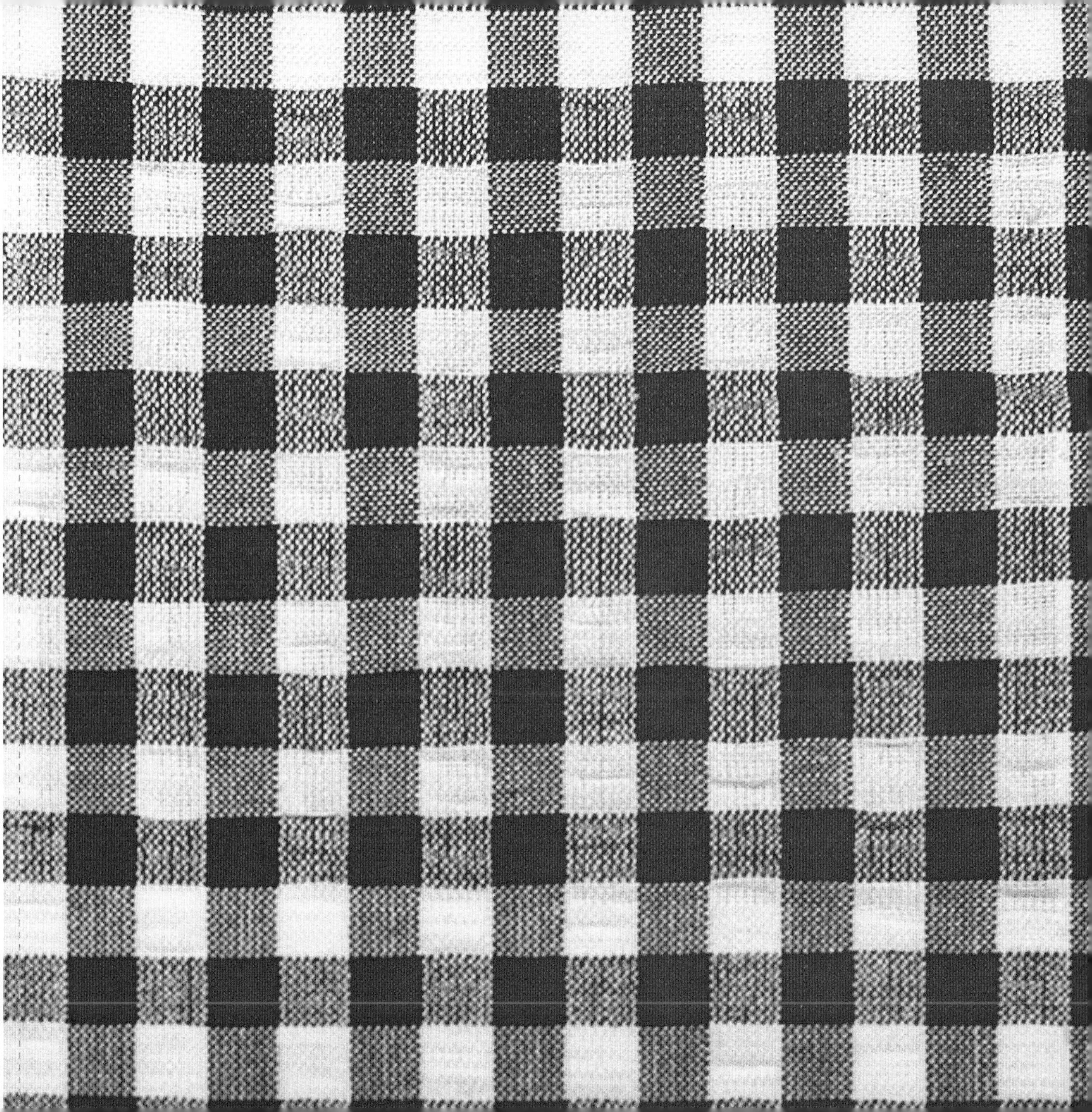

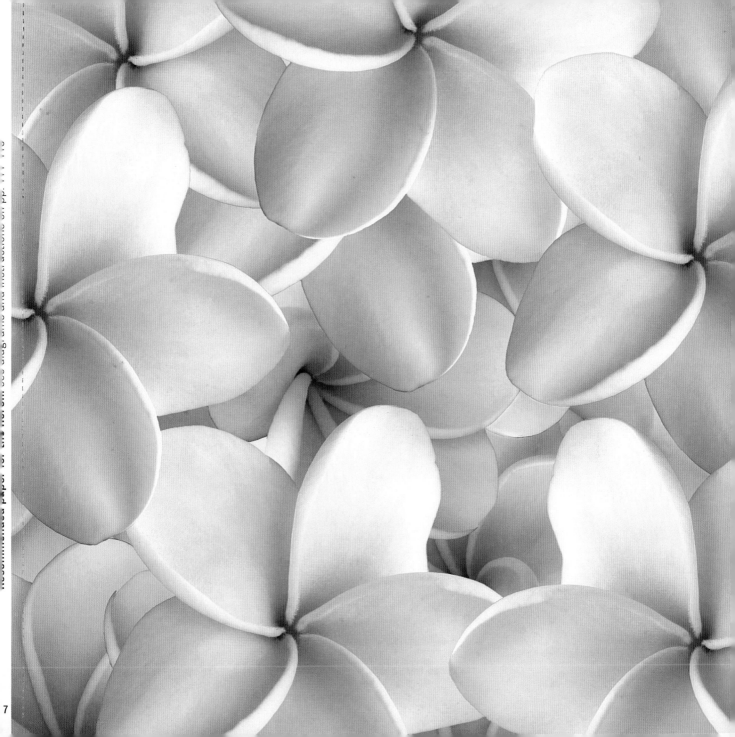

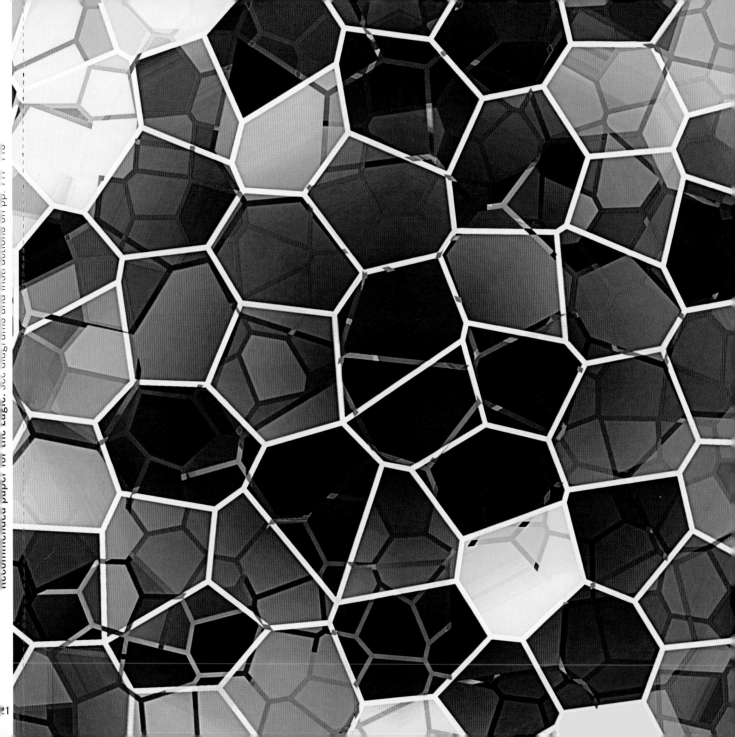

	0697	KAOHSIUNG	1000 095
		HONG KONG	1005 1
	0280	SINGAPORE	1010
	0060	YANGON	1020
D	3771	DUSSELDORF	102
LT	0750	SIEM REAP	1
PG	0931	DUBAI	
CX	0750	HONG KONG	
CX	0713	PHNOM-PENH	
FT	0501	PHNOM-PENH	
KT	0100	MOSCOW	
UN	0523	SINGAPORE	
3K	0511	KUWAIT	
KU	0411	SHANTOU	
	0375	TAIPEI	

1000 1005 1010 1020 102 1

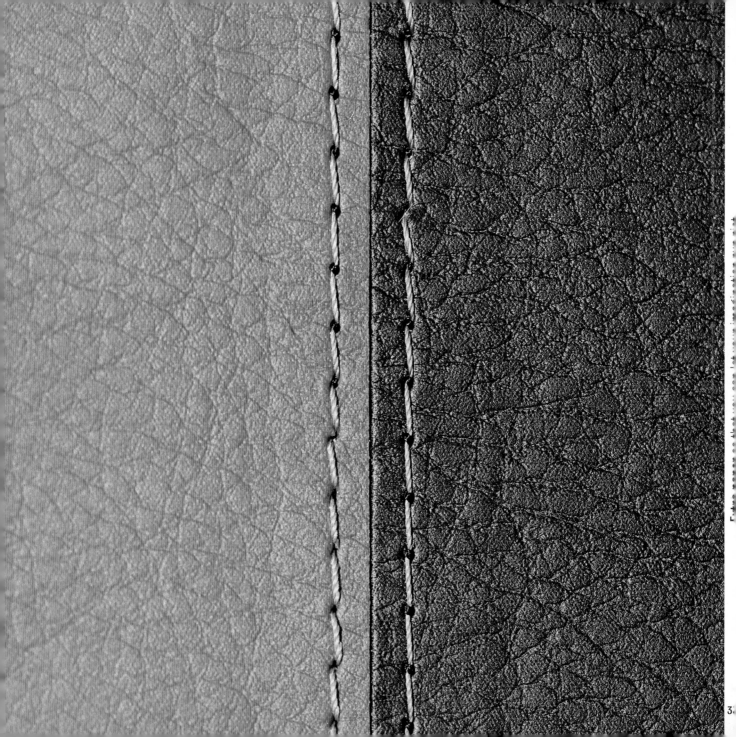

Extra pages so that you can let your imagination run riot